ANGEL
MAGIC

About the Author

Cassandra Eason has been writing about angels for more than twenty years. She lectures, broadcasts, and gives workshops around the world on all aspects of spirituality and magic. She is the international bestselling author of more than forty-five books. Visit her online at www.cassandraeason.com.

To Write to the Author

If you wish to contact the author or would like more information about this book, please write to the author in care of Llewellyn Worldwide and we will forward your request. Both the author and publisher appreciate hearing from you and learning of your enjoyment of this book and how it has helped you. Llewellyn Worldwide cannot guarantee that every letter written to the author can be answered, but all will be forwarded. Please write to:

Cassandra Eason
c/o Llewellyn Worldwide
2143 Wooddale Drive
Woodbury, MN 55125-2989, U.S.A.

Please enclose a self-addressed stamped envelope for reply,
or $1.00 to cover costs. If outside the U.S.A., enclose
an international postal reply coupon.

Many of Llewellyn's authors have websites with additional information and resources. For more information, please visit our website at:

www.llewellyn.com

ANGEL
MAGIC

A Hands-On Guide
to Inviting Divine Help
into Your Everyday Life

CASSANDRA EASON

Llewellyn Publications
Woodbury, Minnesota

First published by Piatkus Books, London, 2009.

FIRST LLEWELLYN EDITION, 2010
First Printing, 2010

Cover design by Lisa Novak
Cover images: background © iStockphoto.com/merrymoonmary;
    feather © iStockphoto.com/Milos Luzanin
Interior illustrations by Llewellyn art department

Llewellyn is a registered trademark of Llewellyn Worldwide Ltd.

Library of Congress Cataloging-in-Publication Data
Eason, Cassandra.
  Angel magic : a hands-on guide to inviting divine help into your everyday life / Cassandra Eason.—1st Llewellyn ed.
     p. cm.
  Includes index.
  ISBN 978-0-7387-2178-1
  1. Angels—Miscellanea. 2. Magic. I. Title.
  BF1623.A53E28 2010
  235'.3–dc22

                          2010023501

Llewellyn Publications
A Division of Llewellyn Worldwide Ltd.
2143 Wooddale Drive
Woodbury, MN 55125-2989
www.llewellyn.com

Printed in the United States of America

To Debbie, my editing angel,
and to my beloved children,
Tom, Jade, Jack, Miranda, and Bill,
who have touched my life with magic.

CONTENTS

INTRODUCTION

The frantic pace of everyday living means that many of us spend our lives in overdrive. People today spend more and more time working, travelling, socialising, and dashing around from home to work and back again. In doing so, we often neglect to stop and reflect on life and on our own physical, emotional, and (perhaps forgotten) spiritual needs. If you want to incorporate spirituality into a busy lifestyle but don't want to commit to a drastic lifestyle change, this book will teach you how to recognise the angels that are all around you and how you can call on them to guide and inspire you in your day-to-day life.

This is not a book about how angels will bring you the winning lottery numbers or return a faithless partner with words of love and red roses. But *you have only to ask* and angels will bring help. Everyone, even the busiest of people, can contact angels and benefit from their help and guidance, without changing their lifestyle or abandoning their beliefs, logic, or common sense. Exploring angel energies, for even five minutes a day, will help you to cope better with daily pressures and move into harmony with yourself and the world around you.

Everyday Angelic Assistance

The word *angel* comes from the Latin *angelus*, which developed from the Ancient Greek word *aggelos* or *angelos*, itself a translation of the Hebrew word *mal'akh*, all of which mean *messenger*. Indeed, there are many accounts of angels delivering messages to help us—sometimes in life-or-death situations, as in the case of John.

John was driving his car down a narrow lane through the Hampshire countryside at a moderate speed. Suddenly he heard a very authoritative voice say, *"Stop."* Surprised, John slammed on his brakes, only to see a milk truck hurtle around the corner at high speed. John would have collided head-on into the truck had he not stopped. He has not heard the voice since.

The majority of accounts are more about subtle signs that reveal the presence of angels in the everyday world, offering reassurance that we are not alone. Many angelic experiences are spontaneous, but as I will show you, it is possible to invite angelic energies into your life. Remember, nothing is too big or too small to call for angelic help.

The angel who answers your spoken (or unspoken) SOS may appear as a stranger who inexplicably disappears after helping out. He or she may actually have been human, sent by an angel. When you work with angel energies, you will occasionally experience this yourself—being in the right place at the right time to help someone you hardly know.

Take the instance of David, who was in his sixties and had just moved to central France. He was alone in the parking lot of a home improvement store, struggling to load a shower cubicle into the trunk of his car. A man in a nearby car came over and offered to help David. He mentioned, in passing, that he was having problems starting his car; little did he know that David was excellent at fixing cars. Soon they were both on their way. Coincidence maybe, but two people struggling in the same place at the same time answering the other's need happens so frequently that one can't help but speculate that the angels may be *helping us to help ourselves*.

Angelic help may also be received as a resource arriving precisely when needed after a cry for help. After angelic intervention, you will generally feel an overwhelming sense of being blessed and cared for, which you do not generally experience following ordinary good luck or coincidence.

Perceiving Angelic Presences

Children whose minds are still spiritually open often see angels, and it has been suggested that their invisible friends may be the form taken by guardian angels in order not to frighten them.

For example, as a young child, Peter talked to an angel he called Raffel, though his family was not particularly religious. When he was four and was taken to a cathedral for the first time, he ran straight to a statue of Raphael and told his mother that it was his angel. He could not read.

Adults who are highly developed spiritually may perceive angels externally, as do many people who are dying or in times of crisis. It seems angels come to our aid when the power of the moment overrides logical blocks that may stand in the way of our innate psychic or clairvoyant sight.

When we first begin to invite angelic energies into our lives, we may see angels entirely within our mind or in very vivid dreams. Many people see light shimmers or beams, and these also announce an angelic presence. In time, as our spiritual vision develops, we may even catch glimpses of these beings of light at quiet moments of contemplation or in a place of natural beauty.

How is this possible? Each of us, however logical and "grounded," has a spiritual spark within that is essentially the same as angelic energy. With practice, we can make our spark grow, helping us become more intuitive and aware of hidden signs and signals in life. Indeed, the eighteenth-century Swedish philosopher Emanuel Swedenborg believed we all have the potential to become angels—not to sprout wings, but to develop ourselves as spiritually focused people while living in the normal, everyday world.

Angels in Religion and Lore

Pre-Christian religions, such as the ancient Persian fire-based religion of Zoroastrianism that flourished during the seventh and sixth centuries BCE, recognised both angelic and demonic beings in the ongoing struggle between good and evil. The ancient Greeks and Romans had their winged deities including Hermes and Mercury; Iris, Greek goddess of the rainbow, was in Christian times made into an angel herself. This influenced the portrayal of winged angels in art form when Roman Christianity finally accepted angels as part of the official Christian faith in 325 CE.

Angels are also important in Judaism and Islam, and similar beings may be found in Buddhist and Hindu spirituality. Two archangels are mentioned in the traditional Old Testament: Michael, the warrior who commanded the heavenly armies, and Gabriel, the heavenly messenger. Two are mentioned in the apocryphal literature, additional Old Testament material not contained in the traditional form of the Bible: Raphael, the healer in the Book of Tobit, and Uriel, protector of Earth, mentioned in the Book of Esdras.

The Church fathers of early Christianity were the first angel researchers. They were influenced by the Hebrew system of angels, which transformed Pagan deities of the people into angels, as Judaism replaced the old religions. The winged messenger Mercury was merged into the personality of the angel Raphael, and so gradually Raphael was given the qualities of the planet Mercury, named after the god because of its swift passage through the skies.

Many historical paintings feature angels visiting aristocratic and wealthy people, mainly because they were the ones who commissioned the paintings. It was during the First World War, when accounts came from soldiers seeing or sensing angels, that it was first acknowledged that angels could and did have a place in the lives of ordinary men and women.

Frequently Asked Questions

Many people have preconceived notions about what angels are. The following frequently asked questions will help you to understand them more fully.

What are angels?

Angels have been around people as part of daily life for thousands of years. Traditionally, they are pictured as winged beings with golden haloes and human features, but altogether more beautiful. Although we may perceive angels as a kind of superhuman being, they almost certainly have never experienced an earthly human life. The presence of angels extends far beyond what might conventionally be called religion, although they have been described in almost every religion in the world. Indeed, many people with no particular faith have encountered angels, sometimes in the most mundane settings such as supermarkets or urban parks.

Angels take many forms as they help in the everyday world, but may in fact exist as spiritual essences or energies, rather than individual beings. As such, they are not limited by the laws of distance and time, as humans are. We cannot be in two places at the same time, but angels do not have such restrictions.

If you doubt the existence of angels in any way, open yourself to the possibility that we are not alone in the universe: ask for spiritual help and support, especially when earthly assistance is slow in coming, and you will be heard.

How do we know angels exist?

No one has yet managed to persuade an angel to enter a laboratory to be weighed, measured, or wired up to machines. Does that mean they are not objectively real? No, because it is a fallacy that only those things that can be subjected to scientific measurement exist. Often, the most profound angelic encounters are, by their nature, not repeatable or even witnessed. Indeed, it is a weakness of modern society that we require proof for those special moments in our life and cannot just appreciate them.

People helped by angels do not have to have an existing belief in angels, nor do they necessarily turn to religion afterwards. You will find many accounts in this book of ordinary people who never go to church, yet who believe that angels have touched their lives and so discovered there is something more to this life than what is immediately visible and material. It is for you to judge the credibility of the experiences in this book and in your own life. As you will see in chapter 1, once you begin to welcome angels into your everyday life, you will be offered small but significant proof of their existence.

What do angels look like?

We tend to interpret angels in a way that is familiar to us, as a kind of superhuman. Indeed, angels may take on superhuman form so we may interact more easily with them, for it would be quite hard to communicate with swirls of light energy. Tradition suggests that angels are androgynous—that is, containing both male and female energies—though we tend to see specific angels as either male or female. This may partly depend on the role of the angel in our lives and whether the angel has predominantly male or female characteristics. Love angels, for example, generally appear feminine whereas angels of courage seem masculine to many people, though of course women can be very fierce and brave fighters and men have gentle, romantic sides.

History has shaped the way angels are perceived, especially during medieval times through to the fifteenth- and sixteenth-century Renaissance and its revival of classical art and sculpture from artists such as Michelangelo. Victorian times gave us sentimentalised romantic angels. However, there is no reason you have to accept any of the descriptions given in this book or in any other book or picture. I suggest you form your own opinions and interpretations of how different angels feel and look as you work with their energies.

A total stranger may turn up, resolve a situation, and then disappear, sent by your angel. This may even be your angel in earthly form. Since angels are not limited to a single physical body, they can appear in ways that are most appropriate to the need. After all, if you were struggling with a heavy burden, people would be astonished to see a white-robed, golden-winged being effortlessly shouldering your bag for you. However, no one would give a second glance to a teenager in ripped jeans with headphones in his ears offering to help and then disappearing into the crowd afterwards.

Does everyone have a guardian angel?

At one time or another, almost everyone has said, "Oh, my guardian angel is working overtime," or, "My guardian angel must have been watching over me." I believe there is a benign spiritual essence or presence with us all. We are all spiritual beings in a physical body, whether or not we believe in an afterlife. It would seem that this inner spiritual part of us is accompanied into and out of life by an angelic presence. For example, sometimes a dying person will see an angel just before death, and at such times the fear of death goes. I have given examples of angelic presences at birth and death later in the book.

The idea of one or more spiritual beings who are always with us may seem strange. Some people imagine their guardian angel is noting down every misdemeanour to be read when we die in some celestial court of law. Angels are not judgmental, however. We all have free will and our guardian angel will not interfere with even the stupidest decisions we make, nor observe us when we would not wish it. They listen like a parent in another room for our cry of distress and come to our aid if called. Some people use their angels as a sounding board and gain responses in all kinds of ways, such as the appearance of white feathers in a totally unexpected place, or suddenly hearing words from a significant song on a radio that answers a question.

Guardian angels help most by providing an earthly means of resolving our own problems, such as a cheque for an unexpected rebate arriving in the post on precisely the day you need it. When such help occurs frequently, at the time and in the way most needed, you start to accept that your guardian angel is looking out for you.

Are there different kinds of angels?

Traditionally there are nine ranks, or choirs, of angels who become more remote from humans the higher they are in the celestial pecking order. Archangels are more powerful than guardian angels and are usually concerned with global issues. However, these higher angels can also be approached directly by any one of us when their particular expertise is required. For instance, if you needed help with a job interview, you could ask for Archangel Sachiel's help. Sachiel is the angel of harvest and abundance and, by association with the Roman god Jupiter, also the angel of justice, employment, promotion, and matters of leadership. He is said to indicate your success if you see any of the following: a purple haze, purple lights, or golden specks of dust when there is no sunshine; a bee entering your home when there are not any around; purple flowers or purple grapes in an unusual setting or context. The closer to your angelic request any of these signs occur, the greater your chance of success.

Do different angels have different functions?

Being a messenger is one of the traditional angelic functions, but angels are so much more than celestial post persons who pass our requests up through an angelic hierarchy to the deity. Your guardian angel is your celestial best friend and always comes to you, even when you have just had a monumental row with your nearest and dearest, eaten a sleeve of chocolates, and felt fat, sick, and unloved by the world.

But many other angels regularly appear in your life. Your healing angel will guide you towards a healthier lifestyle, calm stress, and help your immune system fight illness. Your household angel (in pre-Christian times known as "the guardian of the place") protects you in your home as well as on journeys connected with the family, such as taking children to school. Also, if you have worked in the same place for a year or more, you may get to know the workplace angel. Later in this book, I have listed different angels and their areas of influence. Where relevant, I have described their associated colours, fragrances, and crystals; at the back of the book are 250 angel names and their purposes, to guide you in choosing the right angel for specific needs.

There are angels for every need and situation. However, if you are out and about and you cannot refer to this book, you can ask in your mind for your guardian angel to obtain the necessary assistance for you, and it will come.

What Angels Mean to People with Busy Lives

Angels can lead us to an oasis of stillness and calm even in the most chaotic or pressured situations. This will happen more easily and quickly if we spend quiet times, even ten minutes in a city square at lunchtime, getting in touch with that stillness and angelic harmony so we have a store of tranquillity from our angels that we can call upon in stressful times.

Angels can assist most by helping us to help ourselves, as they did with David in the home improvement store parking lot. They give us strength and confidence, or send along the resources we need to help us cope better. Above all, angels are not there to stop us from making mistakes, for as any wise parent knows, we need to experience life and that sometimes means getting it wrong. Angels can, however, intervene if we really are in trouble and give us a sense of being cared for and loved, as the following case studies will show you.

THE ANGEL OF THE OUTBACK

Lia from Australia told me how in 1984, her twenty-four-year-old brother Gary got lost while on a long run through the Outback and went missing for eleven days. Those of you familiar with the bush land know that even close to a small town, it's quite easy to wander off course, go farther and farther into the scrub, and lose all sense of direction. After a few days of surviving on water and whatever he could forage, Gary was becoming feeble and cold, especially at night, as he was only wearing jogging shorts and a thin top.

One day, Gary was sitting weakly against a tree. Suddenly he became aware of a man in a slouch hat whom Gary says he heard, but never saw properly. The man was leaning up against the other side of the tree. The man told him how to make a fire by rubbing two sticks together and coached Gary through basic bush survival techniques. The man then totally vanished.

Feeling a bit stronger, Gary decided to walk in a particular direction where at last he heard a car, an off-road vehicle carrying two young guys who had gone on a bush trek. They brought Gary to safety.

Of course, sceptics will argue the celestial bush ranger could have been a hallucination due to Gary's weakened condition, but the fact is this mysterious figure helped Gary to survive long enough to be found by two flesh-and-blood rescuers.

THE TRAFFIC ANGEL

Sue from London was on her way to pick up her son Josh after school, and she was running very late. She needed to collect another one of her children elsewhere, so she asked the angels to help her, as she often did. As Sue's car arrived at a narrow junction, she slowed down, expecting the oncoming car to stop, as she had the right of way. The other car, however, did not even slow down. It was rush hour and the traffic was very dense; both Sue and Josh thought that there would be a crash.

What happened next was quite incredible. Both cars were put into reverse and moved backwards, but without hitting the cars behind them. Sue, who was astounded, said that she did not have time to put her car into reverse, and would not have done so because of the cars behind her. The driver's face in the oncoming car was also one of pure shock. Not only that, when Sue arrived safely to pick up her second child, the time registered as the exact time she had arrived to collect Josh.

AMANDA'S BIRTH ANGEL

Amanda from Australia was having a very difficult labour with her second child, and was reaching the end of her coping threshold. The midwife, however, was extremely unsympathetic, and told Amanda to push, but it was before she was fully dilated, causing more pain.

When Amanda felt she could endure no more, a nurse with red hair came into the room, walked straight past the midwife and over to Amanda's side. No one paid the nurse any attention while she leant down and looked into Amanda's eyes and told her in a beautiful calming voice that she had come to help deliver a beautiful and special baby boy. Amanda became calm as the new nurse took over, helping her to breathe. The pain eased and the rest of the delivery passed smoothly. The nurse left, having said her name was Maureen. Amanda's newborn son had the same colour hair as the mysterious nurse.

Once Amanda was home, she wanted to thank the kind helper. She rang the hospital, but they were not able to identify Maureen. Instantly, Amanda *knew* Maureen had been an angel sent to help safely deliver her baby. Amanda says she knew this in her heart and soul because the woman radiated love, compassion, and peace, and no one else in the room had seemed aware of her presence.

In all these stories, help was sent in the way and at the time it was needed. Of course, Amanda cannot prove that Maureen was an angel, but the fact that she felt such wonderful calm and radiance in a crisis suggests that it was indeed an angel who came just when needed. The name Maureen is the Irish variant of Mary, who is called upon by women in childbirth and means *beloved*.

Because so many angel encounters are only experienced by the person being helped, they cannot be verified, but in all cases a sense of a spiritual presence was felt and the results were positive. Sue did not take the number of the approaching car to back up her experience. She just was glad of the help. The bushman, had he been real, would have rescued Lia's brother; but had he appeared in angelic form, Gary might have panicked and maybe thought he had died.

Using the Resources of This Book

Angels will not make all bad things disappear, but they will bring you relief when needed and give you the strength to cope in times of crisis. In the longer term, they can guide you to what your priorities are and help you find real happiness, not just instant fixes.

In the following chapters, I suggest different ways the angels may contact you, and various ways you can contact them, so you can choose the most appropriate method for you. Even if Swedenborg was wrong and we are not all potential angels, we can transmit positive thoughts and actions to help improve our daily lives and the lives of those around us. It may be that a simple smile, just for a moment, has made you the guardian angel of someone who desperately needed a sign of hope.

one

EVERYDAY ANGELS

How many times have you been in a tricky situation and thanked
your lucky stars for the stranger who was passing and happened to be able to help? A few months ago, I accidentally locked
myself out on the balcony of my second-floor hotel room in Egypt
in the middle of the night (I am an insomniac). I asked the angels if
they could possibly send along someone who could help. About five
minutes later, my rescuer, a lady pushing a stroller, came into sight in
the otherwise deserted complex.

Of course my helping angel was human, but she came at the right
time (and an unlikely one) after I had asked the angels for help. However, in other cases I describe in this book, the helper may just disappear and may indeed be an angel in human form.

Some people think of otherworldly dimensions as somewhere
high in the sky or beyond the farthest imaginable galaxy. However,
accounts throughout the ages suggest that angelic realms share the
same space as us, just on a different plane. Scientists are constantly

discovering new energy waves and vibrations. Perhaps angels, along with other beings such as spirit guides and human spirits, exist at an energy vibration not yet discovered or measured. But just because they cannot yet be measured does not mean they do not exist. These energies may be experienced in many other ways in our lives: as vivid dreams, in a near-death experience (see pages 210–212), or simply by becoming aware of shimmering light, hearing tiny bells, or smelling a wonderful but inexplicable fragrance.

Angels may be seen externally or by an inner vision. Many children possess this clairvoyant vision naturally, and to them, seeing an angel externally is commonplace. My son Jack often saw angels as a child and once tried to rationalise the experience by asking me if the angel outside his bedroom window was a clockwork angel. Heidi's young daughter complained to her mother that when she talked to the angels, she could not always hear what they were saying back.

Angelic Help or Coincidence?

Many everyday encounters with angels occur spontaneously, and often it is only the uncanny accuracy of timing and the sense of being blessed and protected that distinguishes the experiences from coincidence. However, angels will give us unmistakable signs of their presence even in mundane situations, and these I have described later in the chapter.

Angelic communications are essentially a two-way process. An angel hears your spoken or unspoken call for help and moves near. You will sense or recognise the angel's presence, maybe as a shimmering light sensation or simply as a human third party helping out.

The following are examples when coincidences may have had some apparent angelic intervention because of the incredible sense of timing. All the people involved have a belief in angels.

MARY AND THE STEEP HILL

Mary from the Isle of Wight had to catch the ferry to Southampton for an appointment, but the parking lot near the port was full so she had to walk more than a mile down a very steep hill.

On the return ferry, Mary discovered she had run out of money, so she could not get a taxi. She said in her mind, *Angels, please help me on this one as there is no way I will get up that hill.* In mid-journey a man sat next to her and she realised it was Neil, a former neighbour whom she had not seen for years. As they were getting off the boat, Neil asked Mary to come and say hello to his wife, Annette, who was collecting him. Mary went with Neil but did not ask for a lift as she was too shy. Yet as they were driving off, Annette suddenly stopped the car and asked if Mary needed a lift anywhere, and dropped her off at her car.

Was this angelic help or coincidence? Of course Neil and Annette were being friendly in offering Mary a lift, but the timing is significant. It was the one time that Mary really needed a lift as her car was so far away. It was the only time Mary could recall the nearby ferry car park being full, and the only occasion on which she had forgotten her debit and credit cards to take out money for a taxi at the port. Again, it was the first time in years Mary had seen Neil. He had come from Singapore and so his timing for the ferry (about sixty miles from the airport) was uncertain, while Mary had missed her intended earlier return ferry by a minute. Neil and Annette lived in totally the opposite direction from Mary. Intriguingly, Mary had helped Annette and Neil's son who had been in trouble when she had met him earlier in the year on another part of the island. It seems that many angel experiences occur with people who help others without being asked and, in doing so, open themselves up to angel energies. Everyone in this case was in the right place at the right time.

JACK'S REUNION

Jack and James, both in their late teens, arrived late at night at a campsite near Barcelona. Jack then realised he had left his passport back in Malaga, so he left his travelling companion and set off on a thirteen-hour bus journey to retrieve it, promising to be back within forty-eight hours. Having taken longer than expected, Jack arrived back in Barcelona five days later. Unfortunately, Jack had no idea of the name of the campsite or even where it was, as he and James had pitched their tent in the dark. Not only that, Jack had also lost his mobile phone and James had left his in England.

So, with not very much money and no way to contact James, Jack decided to walk up the main street, trusting as always that his angels would look after him. After about five minutes, Jack met two people he knew from his home town of Winchester in England, and they invited him to share their hotel room for the night. The next morning he went to a Burger King for breakfast. To his amazement, in walked his travelling companion. James had been frantic and was going to call the police when Jack had not turned up. The amazing thing was that the only reason James was in Burger King was that he needed to go to the toilet; he had gone into Starbucks but the toilet was temporarily closed.

James could have gone anywhere or not have been in town at all, and the odds of James and Jack finding each other in a city of more than a million people by chance was remote. The amazing timing of both Jack's "good Samaritan" rescues was uncanny. By nature, Jack always helps anyone in trouble. In doing so he, too, may have opened himself up to the help of angel energies.

TOM'S NEW SUIT

Tom, a retired Yorkshire vicar, desperately needed a new suit. He had been appointed president of the local Mental Disability Society and his first duty was to attend a charity event at the town hall to accept a cheque from the Lord Mayor on behalf of the Society. Tom's old suit was shabby and he was broke, so he prayed for just enough money to buy a new suit so he would not let the Society down. Each day he looked in vain for a tax rebate or some unexpected cheque. Then, on the day he had to attend the presentation, he found a huge black bin bag of clothes at his front door. This was quite common as people used to leave their old cast-offs for Tom to give to those in need. For the first time ever, Tom tipped the bag out and found a nearly new suit. He was an unusual size and yet it fit perfectly.

THE ANIMAL ANGEL

Donna, who lives in the Midlands, believes angels protected her dogs from a second attack, after one of them had been badly injured several years earlier by an out-of-control Staffordshire bull terrier. After the first incident, Donna continued to walk her dogs on the same route, but was very wary of the breed.

One day in August, Donna's guardian angel warned her not to go the usual way through the woods, so she went in the other direction. Within seconds, as she glanced over her shoulder, two Staffordshire bull terriers were coming out of the woods where she would have normally walked, the owner way behind and not controlling the dogs at all. What confirmed the warning as angelic intervention for Donna was that she saw angel-shaped clouds in the sky.

Ten signs from the angels

People who have studied angels have discovered there are certain ways in which angels make their presence felt. You may have experienced these sensations but not realised their significance. Below are ten of the most common signs to help you to identify the presence of an angel, especially if it is at a time when you have asked for angelic help or you have a dilemma or a decision to make.

1. White feathers

White feathers appear in unexpected places, usually when you have called an angel in your mind or if an angel is trying to attract your attention.

CARRIE

I'd read about angels leaving us white feathers as a sign that they are nearby. I decided to test this out, and was amazed to find feathers in all sorts of unlikely situations whenever I asked. I collected these and placed them in a pretty bag.

One day I went to visit my friend, Barb, who shared my interest in angels and all things spiritual. I told her about the feathers I'd been finding and she surprised me by showing me her own collection of angel feathers. We spent a lovely afternoon talking about angels and, when it was time for me to go home, Barb opened her front door. As we looked out, we both gasped in amazement. Her entire driveway was littered with hundreds of tiny white feathers. We were both thinking "angels" but I said, "Okay, let's be practical and look for the dead bird or some blood." We could find neither. Very strangely, the feathers formed a kind of boundary around her drive— not one feather strayed on to her neighbour's drive or the pavement. We both agreed that it was a strong message from our angels saying, *"Yes, the feathers you've been find-*

ing have been from us." I drove home feeling exhilarated and with the biggest smile on my face ever!

Like Carrie, start a collection of white feathers you find in unusual settings, noting times, places, what was happening in your life at the time, what you were feeling just before you saw the feather, or any pressing questions you needed answering.

When you find a white feather in an unusual situation, sit down and hold it in your cupped hands to activate your sensitive palm chakras (inner psychic energy centres) that are connected with your heart chakra where spiritual information is processed (see the diagram on the following page).

CHAKRAS FOR ANGEL WORK

You do not need to know anything about chakras or spiritual energy work, except that these energy centres are naturally sensitive areas through which angelic energies can enter our body and mind. I will talk about these energy centres more as you work more with angels.

The diagram on the following page shows you where it is believed the four most important chakras are in your body. These upper four chakras are the main ones involved in angel work.

Hold the hand you write with in front of your body around these areas and you may feel a swirling warm sensation coming from these invisible but powerful places of energy. Put your palms together and then move them slowly towards and away from each other. You will feel the build-up of this energy between your palms as if they were being drawn together like magnets.

Upper Body Chakras

Crown: Psychic energy centre we all possess that links us with angelic energies and the light of the cosmos.

Third Eye: Where your clairvoyant (clear seeing) or psychic vision resides.

Throat: Where your clairaudient (clear hearing) abilities are activated; that is, the ability to hear angelic voices or music externally or within your mind.

Heart: Activates claircognisance (clear knowing), which may create a sensation of buzzing or the hair tingling on the back of the neck as your angel approaches. Also clairsentience (clear sensing) or ability to detect angelic fragrances is activated.

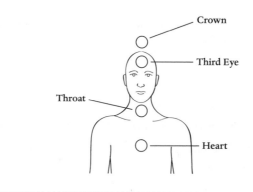

· ·

2. SHIMMERING LIGHT

Shimmering light, dancing light beams, dancing rainbows, silver glitter, or golden dust-beams forming a pattern seen out of the corner of your eye when there is no obvious sunlight. Also a slight buzzing sensation heard and felt within your body with a sense of inexplicable anticipation.

3. ANGEL WINGS

Becoming aware of an angel wing or feeling angel wings touching you, sometimes called an angel hug. Angel wings are the part of the angel that is most visible externally and may be seen as being made of feathers or light. Some people do not see angel wings, but feel themselves hugged or enclosed by the wings, described as the softest blanket imaginable.

4. BELLS

The melodic tinkling of tiny bells, especially in the early morning or late evening when all is silent. This is a very common sign of angelic presence and uses our psychic hearing ability, called clairaudience. If you listen to the bells, they may suggest words in your mind. Often household angels use this method, and they may stop a baby crying with their lovely sounds. The more quiet times you have, however brief, the more you will hear angel music.

5. FLORAL FRAGRANCE

A sudden wonderful floral fragrance more delicate and more beautiful than any earthly perfume, where there were no noticeable fragrances prior to the experience. This is another common way angels make their presence known, and as you work more with specific angels, you will become aware of their different fragrances. Your guardian angel may spontaneously announce his or her presence with a specially sweet or rich form of your personal favourite floral fragrance, again even if you have none of the perfume or oil in the room.

6. BUTTERFLIES

A butterfly or beautiful moth, especially out of season, that flies into your home and settles close to you or remains outside motionless for a long period of time. Butterflies and moths have traditionally been seen as spirit travellers and a way that angels move easily around the earth. Both are symbols of rebirth and transformation so this angelic

signal may appear after a setback, when you are seeking a new beginning, or even around the time of a birth or the death of someone to
whom you were very close. Moths and butterflies are a very subtle
form of angelic communication and they sometimes bring a message from a deceased relative who has been on your mind.

Butterflies are often a way of saying to a person who is always dashing or is a workaholic, "Hey, slow down and be aware of the wondrous
world beyond the computer screen and stressful daily commuting."

7. WARMTH

A feeling of sudden rippling warmth even on a cold day, as if you
were standing by a warm air vent, followed by a sense of total peace
flooding through you. This sensation may occur at a time when you
were panicking or feeling stressed. There is not usually a message,
but a sense of calm, so thank your angel whenever this occurs.

8. CHORAL MUSIC

Full-blown choral type music, maybe just for a minute or two, of
which no one else seems aware. This is rarer and generally indicates
the presence of an archangel, or that you have spontaneously tuned
into higher angelic energies such as the red and gold seraphim, whose
song, according to the Bible, shepherds heard when Jesus was born.

PEGGY

Peggy, who lives in Kent, heard angelic music at the birth
of her only son, Gavin. She described how immediately
after the birth she heard a great burst of music like a *Te
Deum*. The fantastic music was occasionally heard while
she was holding Gavin; he too listened attentively. At last,
Peggy asked a nurse what was upstairs, the place from
where the music came. The nurse said, "Nothing. This is
the top floor."

Birth is a magical time when angels seem to draw near.

Angelic music or angel song may be heard in the home, but more usually in a sacred setting such as a church or cathedral when it is totally
silent, or in a place of great natural beauty during the early morning
or as twilight falls. Choral music seems to manifest to help you when
you doubt the existence of angels, or have for whatever reason lost
your faith in people.

9. Figure of light

Waking from sleep to see a fleeting glimpse of an unmistakeable
figure of light. The transition between sleeping and waking is the
time when the logical mind is least active and so the spiritual self and
clairvoyant vision are more naturally activated. This experience may
be accompanied by an overwhelming but fleeting fragrance.

MINA

Mina is an historian and archivist in Egypt and a Coptic
Christian, but at one point, he was very close to losing his
faith. One night Mina was half asleep when he felt a great
power around him. Suddenly, a very peaceful bright light
and wonderful fragrance filled his room and an angel appeared. Mina talked to the angel for several minutes, although he cannot recall actual words (this sometimes happens after a spontaneous angelic encounter). Afterwards
he felt happy and at peace. He could not see the angel's
features, but says he was surrounded by light. Every night
for a week the angel came to Mina's room, each time accompanied by the same beautiful fragrance.

10. SOMEONE CALLING YOUR NAME

Someone calling your name two or three times in a rich, melodious tone that makes you feel happy and sad at the same time. The voice may sound urgent if you are about to do something stupid or dangerous.

MARGARET'S WARNING

Margaret from Bournemouth was visiting her father in hospital. During the journey home she was very upset and wasn't concentrating. Her car was drifting across the lanes on an urban motorway when suddenly a voice said sharply, *"Get back into lane at once!"* She pulled back instantly into her own lane and narrowly avoided a collision with a car coming up fast on the outside.

Margaret knew it was her guardian angel that she always felt was with her, but that was the only time she had heard him speak.

Whether internal or external, this voice becomes familiar for many people; you may distinguish your helper angels' different voices. When you hear the voice unexpectedly, check whatever you are doing or planning—you may be about to make a mistake.

Now that you've read the preceding list, ask that in the week ahead the angels use some of these ways to let you know they are around you. Be alert for signs that at first may be quite subtle. If you do experience what seems to be an angelic sign, take five minutes to sit quietly and, if appropriate, light a white candle. Ask if the angel or angels present have a message for you.

✣ COMMUNICATING WITH THE ANGELS

Automatic writing is a very powerful angelic tool. Begin with the protective ritual; your angels will not allow anything that could harm you to move close, but at first you may feel reassured if you carry out the simple ritual below.

Protective Ritual

+ Touch the centre of your brow, the area associated with the spiritual third eye or brow chakra (see the diagram on page 20) and say in your mind, "May angels protect me and only what is good and comes from the light enter this place and guide my hand."

  + If you wish, anoint the centre of your brow with a drop of your favourite fragrance.

Automatic Writing

1. Using a green pen and white paper, allow your hand to write words spontaneously without thinking of what you are writing.

   You may feel the hand you write with vibrate slightly and have the feeling that someone is guiding it. This does not mean that you are being taken over by an angel, rather that your hand is transmitting a message via your higher personal angelic connection; you can stop at any time.

2. When you sense your hand slowing, read what you have written. It may be poetry, part of a song, or information that will answer a question or issue that has concerned you or which will offer guidance to a future step.

As you practise tuning into the presence of angels, you will become more aware of angelic presences in everyday situations and you'll wonder if the unexpected help was more than coincidence. Even if this cannot be proved, accept the occurrence as a blessing and these experiences will occur more and more.

two

GETTING TO KNOW YOUR GUARDIAN ANGEL

The most significant angel and the one with whom we can most easily communicate is our guardian angel. You may already know your guardian angel well. If not, as you work through the exercises in this chapter, you will learn to identify your guardian angel by name and establish channels of communication. This means you can talk to your guardian angel in your mind or ask for help absolutely anywhere and any time, even if you only have two minutes before an appointment.

Your guardian angel is never far away and will help you to fulfil your life potential, but because we all have free will, your angel will never interfere with your choices; it will just support you if things go wrong. In a later chapter, you will encounter Metatron (see page 240), tallest of the archangels, who watches over everyone's guardian angels. He is the guardian angel of all guardian angels.

The Guardian Angel at Birth

Everyone, it seems, has a special guardian angel who comes to us before birth then takes us back to our spiritual home when earthly life is over. There are accounts of guardian angels in many religious texts. The New Testament in the King James Bible, published in 1611, refers to the existence of children's guardian angels in the parable of the lost sheep (Matthew 18:10). Jesus says, "Take heed that ye despise not one of these little ones; for I say unto you, that in heaven their angels do always behold the face of my Father which is in heaven."

In the ancient Persian fire-based religion of Zoroastrianism that flourished during the seventh and sixth centuries BCE, Anahita, one of the *yazatas* (the equivalent of angelic beings), was associated with the birth of children and fertility. In the *Hymn to Waters*, Anahita is described as "the life increasing and the holy, the herd increasing and the holy—who makes all females bring forth in safety, who puts milk in the breasts of all females in right measure" (translated in 1898 by James Darmesteter).

Midwives and mothers have frequently detected the presence of a newborn's guardian angel during or even before labour and in the weeks and months after the birth, helping the mother and protecting the little one from harm.

Maria, a midwife working in Arizona, explained, "I have definitely seen golden light surround the emerging baby on several occasions. It is quite an awesome happening to see this light and perceive the beauty and sacredness of birth. It is like seeing through the door into another world."

Carrie, from Oxfordshire, whose experience with the white feathers I described in chapter 1, told me that she often sees tiny dots of light around her infant son, especially when she is settling him to sleep. She also sees a blue light in the bedroom. On one occasion while Carrie was feeding their son, her husband Adam saw a faint blue mist hovering above him. It lasted for about five minutes before fading. Carrie always asks for protection from Archangel Michael and the family's angels every morning.

Sometimes one of the archangels such as Gabriel, who rules over the home and household angels, can act as guardian to a particular child, especially if the mother is very anxious or has been ill before the birth.

Liz, who lives in Australia, was pregnant with her third child and expecting a girl. She was told later in her pregnancy, however, that she was having a boy and she had no name for him. During a guided group meditation the next day, Liz connected with the Archangel Gabriel, the protector and teacher of unborn children. She felt both Gabriel's love and her son's presence very strongly, and told everyone after the meditation that her son's name was to be Gabriel. Liz had a difficult pregnancy emotionally because she had hormonal imbalances, but because of the archangel's reassuring presence, she knew that everything would be fine. Later, Liz discovered Gabriel's name meant *messenger of God* and she says that already, at eighteen months old, her tiny Gabriel has been a messenger of peace to many people in their lives.

Sue, who lives in California, went into premature labour at twenty-two weeks. The doctors managed to stop it and the next morning Sue woke and saw three beings of light. One figure was over her sleeping husband, one was over her own head, and the third over her stomach. She felt each presence was there to take care of her family.

Your Guardian Angel's Name

As we have seen, it is possible to call on particular named angels for guidance and support, but you can also find out the name of your own guardian angel to connect more strongly to him or her. Many angel names come from old Hebrew or Middle Eastern texts and were adopted not only in religious literature, but also used by magicians from the early centuries onwards to invoke angelic energies. Some angel names, therefore, are very hard to pronounce and so many guardian angels use names we can more easily associate with when talking to us. Do not be surprised, then, if your guardian angel uses an ordinary name, maybe one you have always loved. Your guardian angel's name may come to you during a moment of quiet contemplation at your angel place (see page 32), or you can find out the name of your guardian angel using some of the methods I outline on pages 37–41.

Your Own Angelic Name

Some people who work with guardian angels adopt a special name by which their various angels can call them. This name may reflect an aspect of yourself you want to develop, or the softer side of your external competent daily persona. Generally, with less personal angels you use your normal name, just as a bank manager or doctor might address you more formally. It is not necessary to have an angel name, but it does increase the sense of being cherished by your angels, and is most often used with your guardian angel. Indeed, your guardian angel may use a name for you that you were given in childhood, perhaps by a favourite grandmother.

Seeing Angels Everywhere

Guardian-angel experiences have been reported by people of all ages and professions worldwide. The following are just a selection. For most of us, our guardian angel contacts are gentle encounters, but it is life and death experiences that make it easier for those who doubt angels to accept their existence and welcome them into our lives in subtle but equally precious ways.

RUBY'S GUARDIAN ANGEL

When Ruby was seven years old and living in Nevada, her stepmother had to go into hospital unexpectedly. Ruby's aunt Carrie, whose house was on the other side of the city, had promised to collect Ruby from school to look after her. But her aunt was late, so Ruby decided to find her own way. In a few minutes Ruby was completely lost and terrified in an unfamiliar part of town. She prayed for help and a voice told Ruby to follow its sound and she would be shown the way. Ruby stopped being afraid and followed the directions she was being given. She arrived at her aunt's home to find total panic—her aunt was very upset and search parties were out looking for Ruby. No one could believe Ruby could possibly have found her way, as she had not even known the address.

MICHAEL'S GUARDIAN ANGEL

Michael, who lives in Sydney, described how when he was twelve, his father took him on a camping holiday in western New South Wales. They camped in a town where one of his father's friends lived. This friend took them on a tour of some abandoned gold mines, and at one point said that there were no more mine shafts in the area, so it would be safe for Michael to run around. Michael immediately started running towards a low mound, intending to jump from the top, when a voice said, *"Don't jump."* Michael ignored the voice and kept running. The voice came a little louder: *"Don't jump."* Puzzled, Michael looked around but could not see anyone. He kept running, but this time he felt a hand on his chest and the voice spoke even more clearly, *"DON'T JUMP."* This time Michael took notice, stopped running, and walked up the gently sloping mound to discover the gaping hole of a mine shaft. If he had kept running, he would have fallen into it.

Connect with Your Guardian Angel

There are some simple techniques you can learn in a few minutes to find out who your guardian angel is and, more importantly, how to *feel* him or her. I will show you how to create an "angel place" in your home that will help you connect with your guardian angel on a regular basis. With practice, you can do this in even the noisiest of households, but at first it is best to be in a quiet space (if necessary, use ear plugs or headphones playing soft music).

Your angel place

You probably already have most of what you need to set up your angel place, but as you develop your work with angels you may wish to add items I have marked with an asterisk. (*)

Set up your angel place on a table in a corner of your home or maybe in your garden, perhaps in a garden shed—anywhere to serve as your special "time out" area. A home with an angel place seems to transmit calming or healing energies, and people will comment how light and welcoming it feels.

You will need:

+ A table covered with a white cloth
+ A large white candle, scented or unscented, placed in the middle of the table
+ A statue of an angel (which could be made of any material) placed next to the candle*
+ At least two forms of angel fragrance (see page 33), for example, fresh flowers or a growing pot herb, incense sticks, potpourri, essential oils, or scented candles
+ A green ink pen and white paper or an unlined notebook
+ A pointed clear quartz pendulum*
+ A small quartz crystal sphere. This should not be totally clear but have lines, flaws, and cloudy areas within it*
+ A small bowl of angel crystals (see page 35) and one or two larger ones. Try to choose at least three different kinds, as you may find one particular crystal works well with your guardian angel

If you are new to working with angels, simply having the angel place in your house can help you to attune to the energy of your guardian angel. It provides a quiet, calming place to reflect on whatever's happening in your life, and sitting and reflecting in your angel place will bring you inner peace to counteract a stressful daily life. For some people, creating the angel place will be sufficient to permeate your home and your own energy field with a sense of harmony and of being blessed. However, once you feel ready, you can use your angel place as a focus to initiate contact with your guardian angels, should you need their guidance or extra support in any aspect of your life.

Always begin by lighting your candle and either a fragrance oil or your incense stick, even if you are only sitting quietly in the angel place and not doing any active angel communication.

As you light your candle, ask that your special guardian angel draws close and that they make their presence known to you in a way that will help you make the connection.

Angel fragrances

Fragrance is an easy and very direct method of connecting with angel energies. In chapter 1, I explained how your four upper chakras were the places that you could use fragrance to link with angel experiences (see the diagram on page 20 as a reminder). You can use floral perfume, scented water, or an essential oil diluted well in almond or virgin olive oil. Aerosols are not suitable.

Try these fragrances individually, or mix them up to attract angelic presences:

Apple blossom	Honeysuckle	Lilac
Mimosa	Violet	Carnation
Hyacinth	Lily	Neroli
Geranium	Jasmine	Linden blossom
Orange blossom	Hibiscus	Lavender
Lotus	Rose	

You may find others scents work well for you, and if you love the outdoors, tree fragrances such as cedar, pine, and juniper may evoke beautiful, strong green nature angels. Alternatively, at first, you can use your favourite fragrance, even if it is not primarily floral. Keep this in the centre of your angel place to empower it. Often your guardian angel's spiritual fragrance is remarkably similar to your favourite fragrance, but altogether richer and more beautiful. If, however, you smell an altogether different fragrance when you know your angel is near, you can shop around for a perfume or essential oil that is very similar to that. Again, keep it on your angel table to empower it. Then, when you are ready, follow the directions below to anoint your upper chakras, which will open you to the presence of your guardian angel.

1. With a single drop of the fragrance on the index finger with which you write, anoint the centre of your hairline where it meets your forehead to access the inner crown chakra. Rub in the fragrance anticlockwise if you are a woman, clockwise if you are a man (this applies to all the anointing rituals described below). You may feel warm light flowing downwards into your body through this energy centre.

2. With a second drop of perfume or oil, anoint the centre of your brow, your third eye or brow chakra. You may experience light, shimmering rainbows, or golden specks of dust that appear in front of or out of the corner of your eyes and just as rapidly disappear.

3. With a third drop, anoint the hollow of your throat (throat chakra). You may hear your guardian angel speaking to you in a voice you recognise in time as distinctively theirs. However, many people hear angelic words as their own inner voice but adapted with different speech patterns and phrases. Others just *know* instinctively what the angels are saying. All these clairaudient, or hearing, sounds from other dimensions are activated through your sensitive throat energy centre.

4. Finally, put a drop of fragrance on each of your inner wrist
    pulse points. This connects with the heart chakra where all
    the spiritual energies from the earth and the cosmos meet and
    mix, including your psychic touch, or psychometric potential
    (the ability to divine information through touch).

Angel crystals

Crystals are another great tool to initiate contact with your guardian
angel. Here is a list of crystals that seem to work particularly well.

SMALL POLISHED ANGEL CRYSTALS INCLUDE:

Deep purple amethyst
Medium-blue angelite with veined blue wings
Green or purple semitransparent fluorite
Herkimer diamond
Translucent cream rainbow moonstone
Clear crystal quartz
Rutilated quartz filled with yellow or brown needles, known
    as angel hair
Softly transparent pink rose quartz
Deep blue and white or indigo sodalite

LARGER OR ANGULAR CRYSTALS INCLUDE:

Celestite: a pale-blue egglike crystal made up of clusters of
    smaller blue crystal chippings that may contain holes or
    doorways, through which in time you may see angelic
    realms. You can also buy small polished round blue celes-
    tite for your crystal bowl.

Opal aura crystal or angel aura crystal: comes in large or
    small pieces of varying shapes. You do not need a large
    piece as it is so potent for angel work and each piece is
    said to contain its own guardian spirit. Apart from a clear

quartz crystal sphere, this crystal is probably the most effective guardian angel crystal.

However, as with fragrances, if you have a favourite crystal or gem in a piece of jewellery that is not listed, this could be your guardian angel crystal as it will be very connected emotionally to you. Some people light a fragrance such as an incense stick, oil, or scented candle, or anoint themselves and then work with angel crystals, so building up and combining the energies.

WORKING WITH ANGEL CRYSTALS

1. After lighting an angel fragrance and a candle in your angel place, hold your favourite small angel crystal between your cupped hands and close your eyes. If you have bought several kinds of angel crystals, try one at a time. One may instantly give you a mental image or a sensation that your guardian angel is present.

2. Open your eyes, look into the candle flame, and you may momentarily see your angel around the halo of the flame. Some people always see the angel in their mind, and this is just as effective.

3. Put down the small crystal and thank your angel. Blow out the candle and sit absorbing the incense or oil fragrance for a few more minutes, allowing information about *your* angel to flow into your mind. This will happen totally spontaneously even if you did not see an angel externally.

If you have a clear crystal sphere:

1. Hold it up to the candlelight or to natural light and look into it. I would recommend this method if you can buy even a small sphere, as it creates almost instant angelic connections and visions.

2. Relax your eyes. Looking at the cracks and lines within the crystal sphere, you may see a quite small but clearly visible image of your guardian angel.

3. When the image fades, close your eyes and allow the image to reappear in your mind, still holding the crystal sphere between your hands to make the connection. Then open your eyes and look into the sphere again and you may see a clearer image of your angel. Close your eyes once more, keeping hold of the sphere. Open your eyes slowly and look beyond the sphere towards the candle and you may see a light shimmer or even momentarily your angel.

4. Finish by thanking your angel, as above.

Repeat the session weekly and you may find that when you pick up the crystal or sphere, you know instantly what your angel is saying, and can enter a dialogue in your mind.

In time, as you become more experienced, you can make the connection anywhere and instantly, without even using the crystal. However, some people do carry a guardian angel crystal in a small purse and hold it or touch the bag to make the connection when daily life becomes stressful. They can connect you with angels anywhere, on the train or while you are preparing notes in the office for a meeting.

Ask Your Guardian Angel

Although sometimes you just want the support of your guardian angel—to know they're there looking out for you—other times you may need guidance on specific issues. While working at your angel place is a good way to connect with your guardian angel, my favourite tool for asking questions or receiving advice from my guardian angel or other helping angels is to use a clear crystal pendulum. The pendulum movements act as external confirmation of what you may hear in your mind, but may not fully trust as angelic wisdom.

Using a pendulum for angel communication

Crystals and clear quartz in particular are natural amplifiers and transmitters of spiritual energies, and a pendulum by its movement offers confirmation of information that you may doubt. Stephanie, a young businesswoman working in a very competitive finance environment, often consults her pendulum if she feels overwhelmed by the pushy attitudes of a few older colleagues who resent her early success. After a meeting, she slips into the restroom and holds her pendulum for a minute or two. She asks her guardian angel if a decision she is being pressured into is right. This is invariably a situation in which Stephanie has doubts about her colleagues. The pendulum movements usually help to confirm Stephanie's own wise instincts and restore her confidence.

PROTECTING YOUR PENDULUM FROM NEGATIVITY

Working with pendulums to communicate with angels can remind some people of using a Ouija board. However, this is very different from using a Ouija board for calling up spirits, a practice that is psychologically and psychically dangerous. Nevertheless, in order that you feel 100 percent secure it is an angel to whom you are talking, before beginning any pendulum work, light your angel candle and incense and then hold your pendulum a safe distance above the candle flame. Say aloud, or in your mind if you wish, *"Angels, guardians, and guides, may this pendulum be used only by my angels to transmit goodness and light. May anything that is not of light and beauty depart from this place."* Put a pinch of salt in the flame for purification. You could repeat the words and imagine the flame whenever you are making pendulum choices.

....

Using a pendulum to make choices

At first, work with your pendulum in your angel place at a time when you are feeling relaxed and unhurried. If you have not used pendulums before, this will help you to tune into pendulum energies as a transmitter of both your own inner wisdom and as confirmation from your guardian angel of the rightness of those instincts. In time, your pendulum in its simpler yes/no modes of answering can travel with you in your bag or in a small velvet bag in your purse or wallet, as Stephanie's does.

You can use your pendulum to differentiate between a number of choices when you are not sure which option is right or your logical mind or other people are casting doubts. Begin by using the pendulum choice method to guide you in your angel work.

✺ ANGEL CHOICES
....

This method can be used initially to find out more about your guardian angel, such as its preferred crystals or fragrances, but as you progress you can use it to help you decide when you face any choice in your life.

+ Pass your crystal pendulum over a list of fragrance names, alphabet letters set in a circle, letters facing upwards, or over a set of individual crystals. The pendulum will then indicate what is the name and preferred crystals or fragrances of your guardian angel and other angels you encounter.

+ The pendulum will vibrate so you not only see the crystal moving, but feel it in your fingers and hand. The pendulum may also become heavy and even physically pull down towards individual letters or the right crystal.

Each person feels the *"this one"* response sensation differently, but it is unmistakeable when it happens. The sensation is different from a normal yes/no pendulum swing. To practise, try writing several house names or numbers including your own house in separate areas of a piece of paper and ask the pendulum to pull down over the name of your house.

For specific responses from the angels on any issue, you can try the following technique. It can also be used to find or confirm your own angelic name or that of your guardian angel. This is not a psychic test, so you cannot cheat—it is simply a way of getting or confirming information.

FINDING SPECIFIC INFORMATION

1. Write all the letters of the alphabet on squares of white paper or use index cards. Shuffle or mix them and put them in a circle, with the letters facing upwards.

2. State what it is you want to discover. Pass your pendulum slowly clockwise a few centimetres over each letter in turn. Some people prefer to make a complete circuit with the pendulum over all the letters in order first, to tune the pendulum into the energies. The pendulum will indicate by vibrating and/or by pulling downwards towards the individual letters in the name, sometimes the same letter more than once.

3. When no more are indicated, write down the letters in the order they were picked and if necessary rearrange them. There may be vowels missing as in some early languages (especially mystical ones) vowels were not used, but usually the name is instantly quite clear. You can use the same method to discover your own angelic name as well as the names of your household and healing angels when you work with them in future chapters.

You can also write a list of fragrances or colours or make a circle of the actual crystals you own and ask your guardian angel which is best to communicate with. Then you can instantly connect by lighting an appropriately coloured candle or carrying a guardian angel crystal to work. Even if you only have a few crystals, your ever-obliging guardian will choose one as a calling signal.

. . . .

The "yes" or "no" response

A pendulum's yes/no response will give you an answer to direct questions. You can decide in advance the movements for *yes* and *no*; for example, actually making a clockwise circle with the pendulum to stand for *yes* and making an anticlockwise circle for *no*. You say in your mind or aloud, *"When the answer is yes, make this movement"* as you make the clockwise circling movement several times. Do the same for the *no* direction. Pendulums have no independent life of their own and so you can determine the best response for you. The pendulum will then give the appropriate response to a question. When you are working with a guardian angel, you will allow your guardian to guide this movement in order to communicate with you. If you do not give your angel or indeed any other angel permission to do this, they will not impose their will on yours.

Alternatively, you can write the words *yes* and *no* on two pieces of paper and use the earlier pendulum choice method so the pendulum will pull down over the correct one.

✸ USING THE YES/NO RESPONSE

When questioning angels with a pendulum, you may experience a number of feelings: warmth; certainty; as if someone is gently moving your hand or the pendulum; and the sensation as if talking to a wise friend or teacher. You may even hear in your mind the words *"this one"* over the correct choice.

1. After lighting your candle and incense in your angel place, sit quietly for a moment and make an initial connection by holding an angel crystal or your crystal sphere.

2. Then pass the crystal pendulum clockwise round the candle flame three times and ask for the wisdom and protection of the angels to be with you. Ask your guardian angel to guide the pendulum movements.

3. Hold the pendulum in the hand you write with a few centimetres above the table. Ask aloud or in your mind any question you have for your guardian angel about any matter that concerns you. You might ask your angel questions such as "Should I change my job?" or, "Is this person right for me?"

4. The stronger the swing towards *yes* or *no*, the more definite the message. By asking a series of questions, each dependent on the previous answer, you can gain a lot of information from your yes/no movements.

Calling your guardian angel on the move

There are many ways of contacting your angel, but you're not always at home near your angel place when you need assistance. The following are very common and easy ways of calling your guardian angel at any time and any place:

- Hold in your cupped hands your guardian angel's special crystal (which you could carry in a little purse), close your eyes just for a few moments, and ask for your guardian angel to help you or be with you. This you can do most places as you can keep the crystal in the purse.

- Touch your heart or your brow with the index finger of the hand you write with or, if you can, rub a little perfume in the centre of your brow or forehead for your uppermost crown chakra, or on your inner wrist points for the heart chakra. I do this with a rose perfume stick, and if anyone asks, I say I have a slight headache.

- Create a few words you can repeat in your mind that, as well as calling your angel, may actually calm you by recalling the angel energies within you—for example, your angel's name or identification, such as *"My blue angel, come to me, be with me, and comfort me."*

- Wear a special pendant, necklace, bracelet, or ring, preferably with a blue stone, such as a small sapphire. Touch the necklace or the stone in it and call your angel.

three

HOME ANGELS

In addition to our guardian angel, each one of us has "helper" an-gels, who have specific functions in our lives. The most significant of these helpers is your home or house angel, who protects your home, family, pets, and any land you have.

In pre-Christian times, the angels of the home were regarded as land guardians. The belief in house and home guardians still exists in some countries, especially in eastern Europe, the Baltic regions, Russia, and Scandinavia. Few people in modern rural Sweden will under-take renovations without asking the permission of the house spirit. In Iceland, official road planners will go round a land-guardian rock rather than move it, and certain fields are regarded as sacred and so are never used for housing or industry.

Christianity acknowledged these protective domestic energies and assigned particular angels and archangels to watch over the home. The following list is by no means comprehensive, but these are the home guardians still most invoked in today's world:

- **Gabriel**, the silvery archangel of the moon, rules over all individual household angels and homes
- The fiercely protective archangel **Chamuel** or **Camael** protects your boundaries
- Green-robed **Derdekea** guards home, family near and far, land, pets, and property
- **Menadel**, with his silvery light, guides you and loved ones home each night
- **Yeiayel** is the angel of the loving family. He encourages family members to support one another and mends family quarrels

Each home has its household angel and even if you have never consciously connected with yours, you may have sensed their protection at times, perhaps as you looked in your bag for your door key when you got home late at night. Household angels tend to bring practical help but are also very protective of children, and will often comfort a child who is distressed or afraid and who wakes in the night.

THE SNOW-CLEARING ANGEL

Sarah lives in central Sweden. She senses a presence watching her when she goes outside late at night with her dog, making sure she is safe. One night it had been snowing very heavily and the snow was piled up on the steps. Sarah decided to clear it the next day, but when she returned with the dog a path had been cleared for her and the snow was neatly piled up on either side of the steps. She was alone in the house apart from her children who were asleep upstairs.

THE COMFORTING ANGEL

When Mary from New Zealand was eight, she and her siblings had to stay with her grandparents while her mother was in hospital giving birth to another baby. Mary did something that made her grandfather cross and he shouted at her, so she ran into the bedroom and cried herself to sleep. Mary woke in the darkness and there was a beautiful glow around her and someone stroking her. She looked up and saw a lovely woman dressed in white with golden hair. Mary ran out to find her grandparents, and her grandfather simply smiled and asked her if she had seen someone. Mary felt calm, happy, and relaxed.

The next day, Mary's grandfather took her for a walk and apologised for shouting. She told him she really had seen a figure; he replied that the household angel always came to those who needed her help.

THE ANGEL WHO BROUGHT
MUCH-NEEDED MONEY

When Pauline was thirteen, her father had been unemployed for some time. His only boots were worn out. Pauline had been sent to buy bacon and she was worrying about her father having no shoes. The pavement had weeds growing through the cracks. A clear loud voice said, *"Look down among the dock leaves and you will find sixpence."*

Pauline knelt down and felt around the green clumps, but no money was there. Then she saw dock leaves growing out of the wall. She felt carefully around each leaf until at last she made contact with a silver sixpence. Pauline went home with a large bag of bacon pieces and a small ham joint, enough to feed the family for two days.

Pauline told her parents she had found the sixpence, but not about the voice. The angelic find freed enough money for her father to repair his boots, and soon afterwards he got a job.

THE LIFESAVING HOUSEHOLD ANGEL

Cathy and her husband were missionaries in Punjab, India. One night, Cathy put their two-year-old son, Thomas, to bed as usual. After a while she went in to see if he was asleep, but Thomas had crawled down to the other end of the bed. She moved him back with his head on the pillow and went out. A little later the same thing happened, so she moved him back again. A few minutes later, there was a tremendous crash. A cornice of the ceiling had fallen on to Thomas's pillow. The child was unhurt, however, as once again he had crawled (or maybe had been moved by the household angel) to the other end of the bed.

Of course, there is no hard evidence that it was the protector of the household who was watching over the child, but Cathy regarded her son's sleeping position as unusual that night.

ANGELIC CRYSTALS AND FRAGRANCES

As we work with more and more specific angels, I will be adding optional angelic fragrances and crystals. In earlier chapters, I described angel crystals such as angelite or rose quartz, as these do seem to offer an instant connection with angelic energies generally. In this chapter, I add other crystals that work well in specific areas, such as sleep. Of course, there is overlap; rose quartz is a general angelic crystal that seems to call any angels as you hold it, but also promotes peaceful sleep and so can be used in conjunction with sleep angel energies.

The meanings and uses of different crystals have been determined over hundreds of years by traditional writings that are themselves based in uses a number of people have found effective for specific crystals. You can always use the angel crystals listed in chapter 2 not only for calling angels, but indeed for any angelic purpose. But throughout the book I list specific crystals that work extra well for different angels (like fine-tuning the energies); for example, sparkling orange or clear crystals and gems for Michael, archangel of the sun.

I have therefore described below crystals that are fine-tuned for domestic purposes (with or without angels) but which are greatly strengthened by household angelic presences, in this case the angel of your household. Indeed, all crystals have practical uses but in every case, their powers are made especially powerful by angels who rule over the same areas of need as the crystals.

The same is true for fragrances, so that roses will help to connect you with any angel but are specifically helpful for healing or love purposes—and when associated with a love or healing angel such as Anael, archangel of love, marriage, and natural growth, then its power is greatly increased.

Contacting Your Household Angel

If you are in tune with your household angel, whatever your family situation, domestic life tends to run far more smoothly. If, for example, you are carrying out renovations, explain to the angel what you are doing and why; afterwards plans tend to go well and home improvement efforts become less stressful because you are working in harmony and with the blessing of the house guardian.

+ Call on your household angel to bless any family gatherings or events. Ask them also to restore and maintain harmony when troublesome relatives or neighbours visit, or if a member of your household is being difficult.

+ Ask your household angel to protect your home from burglary or vandalism. Your household guardian will also try to keep your home safe against natural disasters, though they cannot stop destructive upsurges of earth power. I have, however, encountered experiences from people who have asked their angels for help when a natural disaster was imminent and their house was the only one virtually untouched in the neighbourhood.

+ When a domestic crisis arises, however trivial, ask your household angel to help you and / or to send some human aid. Crises can include any situation, from a washing machine flood to a ruined meal.

Angela's oven had blown a fuse and the meal she had prepared for her partner's boss was not cooked, so she called on her angels. Her partner's boss phoned very apologetically and said he and Angela's partner had been detained on the other side of town and asked if she would mind getting a taxi at his expense so he could buy them dinner instead.

So many times a solution matches the dilemma and almost always after asking, your household angel helps. The more this occurs, the more you trust the angels, and the more help arrives when needed.

The angelic heart of your home

In addition to your special angel place, you can create a domestic angelic focus in the centre of your living room, to connect with your household angel energies. This will also bring an oasis of peace to even the most frantic home.

YOU WILL NEED:

+ **A low coffee table with candles** (golden, yellow, orange, or beeswax), one for each family member, even if they now live somewhere else.

+ **A statue** that represents for you the heart of your home and the angel who protects it and / or a small rock or unpolished crystal that is traditionally used as a household guardian's symbolic home. Walk in the park or countryside and look for a special

stone, one that stands out from the others, perhaps it glints in
the sun, or is a different colour or shape to those around it.

+ **Little bowls of fresh and dried fruit,** seasonal seeds, nuts, and
berries, so that when people eat them, they absorb the angelic
energies. Replace and top up these dishes regularly.

+ **The fragrances** associated with home angels may be naturally
occurring household smells, such as baking bread even if no
one is cooking, or lavender polish which you can use to evoke
their presence. You can identify your household angel's special
calling fragrance if, for example, you suddenly smell baking
bread and are instantly filled with a sense of warmth and peace,
sensing the angel's presence. Each household angel will have its
own homely fragrance, often one you recall with pleasure from
your childhood. However, you can also call your household angel in times of need with a rose, chamomile, or lavender-based
potpourri rather than with incense or burning oil.

+ **One or more small bowls of crystals** (you need not buy these
all at once) to improve the angelic energies around your home.
These include purple amethyst to guard against all forms of
negativity; sparkling yellow citrine, green jade, black jet, pink
rose quartz, and blue lace agate for kindness and any of the
brown or sandy banded or patterned agates for balanced emotions. You can also carry one of your household angel crystals
with you when you travel to set up a heart of the home in an
unfamiliar hotel or on holiday.

ASK FOR ANGEL PROTECTION

1. When you can, light each person's candle for a few
minutes any time a family member comes home.
Also, light candles if any family member is staying
away overnight or living away from home. This helps

increase the angelic energies around each person. If
you live alone, have one candle for yourself and, if you
wish, add candles for close friends and family.

2. As you light the candle or candles, ask the household
   angel to protect your home and make it a place of
   happiness and harmony.

3. Transfer the candles to the meal table and after the
   meal, blow them out, giving thanks for the meal.

Once a week, try to spend at least half an hour after eating, either
alone or with other family members, in your household angel centre in quiet contemplation and listening even to the youngest family
member.

Identifying your household angel

You may become quite naturally aware of the identity, personality,
and appearance of your home angel by sensing him or her, or you
can use any of the ways I have already suggested in chapters 2 and 3
to supplement your intuitive impressions.

If you want to *see* your domestic angel externally, the easiest way is
to use an ordinary mirror, large enough to see your head and shoulders with a space behind you. Hang it on a wall or prop it up on a
table, facing a blank, preferably light-coloured wall.

1. Light candles: soft natural daylight is best but if the day is dull,
   light lavender, rose-scented, or beeswax candles, so that the
   candlelight reflects within the mirror but you cannot see the
   actual candles in the glass.

2. Relax, half-close your eyes, and ask that your household angel
   will give you an indication of its presence. If you have already
   discovered your household angel's name, call him or her using

this name. Otherwise say, *"Kind angel who protects my home, give me a sign of your presence."*

You may be rewarded by a shimmering image within the mirror or feel a light cool breeze even though there is no source of moving air. You may feel a light featherlike touch on your arm or cheek.

3. Look into the mirror, still through half-closed eyes. Ask if your angels will show you a glimpse of themselves. Now close your eyes, counting slowly from ten down to one in your mind.

4. Open your eyes and blink—and over your right shoulder, you may see your household angel very fleetingly. If you want to call the image once more, shut your eyes, count upwards from one to ten, and then open them again. Do not blink and the image may remain longer, this time smiling.

If this does not work the first time, repeat this up to three times, one after the other.

WHAT IF I SEE NOTHING?

+ It may be your logical mind blocking the process. In this case, look directly into the glass with eyes open while you count down from ten to one even more slowly.

+ Close your eyes and picture yourself in your mind looking into the mirror and seeing your reflection, and to your right side your angel will appear in your mind's vision. Once you have an image, open your eyes, imagine the angel within the glass, and it may appear.

+ Your domestic angel may not look like an angel at all. They are often a very homely and slightly older person dressed in the colours of autumn, surrounded by a rich green or golden brown glow.

Keep practising. Once you have seen or sensed your angel's appearance, you may perceive him or her out of the corner of your eye in the early morning or evening light when the house is quiet, although don't worry if you don't experience this—some of the best clairvoyants and angel channellers only ever see images in their mind's eye.

House-Moving Angels

Household angels tend to remain with a particular property or location, so they can be a key factor in helping a home move go smoothly.

You may view a prospective house or apartment and know instantly it is for you, yet there may be all kinds of obstacles in the way. To obtain the property, ask in your mind when you visit the premises if the angel of the new home will help you to move there. Promise in return to care for the house. If the angel likes you and wants you to live there, the necessary factors will start to fall into place.

Equally, you need to explain to your current home angel why you are moving. The cooperation of the house angel may speed a sale or deliver the perfect new tenant.

Angelic help to find a property

+ If you cannot find the right property, write on a piece of paper precisely what you want, the location and the price you can afford, or use a printed image, maybe from a real estate agent's website or advert. Fold this and put it under your guardian rock or statue on your household angel table. Light a candle and ask for help to find the right new home by connecting with the angel of the place that you are looking for.

+ When you finally move, thank your current household angel and, in order to get to know the new one, take a small plant or two from your old home as a token of your intention to care for the new house. Leave the guardian stone in the garden of your old home.

Kitchen and Mealtime Angels

Food has from time immemorial been regarded as sacred because it is essential to life. Until about fifty years ago in the Westernised world, almost every household said "grace" to give thanks for a meal, even if they were not conventionally religious. However, with the take-out culture and frantic 24/7 pace for many, mealtimes have become fractured with family members eating at different times.

Cooking, too, with a hungry family waiting or perhaps needing to go out again almost immediately can spoil any pleasures in cooking and meal preparation. This is where the angels who preside over mealtimes and the kitchen can bring calm and restore pleasure. These angels do not demand haute cuisine and will help you even if you are microwaving meals or stirring a ready-made sauce into five-minute pasta.

JENNY'S ANGELIC MEALS

Jenny has three children who are fussy eaters and a stressful job. For her, evening meals were a nightmare. Most nights she ended up throwing away most of the meal. Jenny did not even realise she had a household angel, but sent out a general distress call. The message came, "*Talk it through.*"

So the next night Jenny served bread, cheese and fruit and sat the family round the table. Instantly, she felt a new calm as if someone was sitting in the empty fifth chair at the head of the table. Jenny asked the children what the best solution would be, and it was agreed the four of them would spend part of Saturday evening, when they were always home, planning meals for the week ahead, and that it was the job of the children to agree in advance what they would all eat each day. The children also agreed to help prepare these meals, which could be frozen and just reheated quickly. There were no miracles, occasionally some very odd combinations of food and, of course, there were

still arguments. But Jenny says she feels the calming presence in the fifth chair (a chair she had contemplated throwing out after her husband left) and mealtimes are generally
much happier.

Every occasion on which a family or friends gather round the table
is an act of blessing that calls down the angels concerned with food
and food production. I have listed below only angels concerned with
the home directly, but Sachiel, the archangel of abundance and the
harvest, may be helpful, especially when fixing larger celebrations.

Mealtime angel names

Jophiel, the sunshine-yellow archangel with his orange halo,
blesses mealtimes as one of his many functions.

Isda, motherly angel of nourishment, carries a basket of
bread. She says you must care for yourself and your own
needs as well as others.

Lecabel, angel of food and the family table, blesses your
mealtimes and your kitchen.

Manna, angel of food, ensures there are sufficient resources
for the home if you call on her, and so she is good if you
have a very tight budget. She also blesses family celebrations or gatherings. Her name was given to the food of
the angels that was occasionally offered to mortals.

Seheiah, or **Sealiah,** protects you in the kitchen against
burns, cuts, and spills, and also from bacteria and food
hygiene-related germs.

Shekinah is the angel who traditionally lights the Sabbath
candles in Jewish homes at dusk on Friday evenings,
through the hands of the mother or eldest daughter. However, she will be present on any day of the week and at any

meal in any home whenever you light a candle and ask for blessings, whatever your beliefs about the nature of divinity or the powers of goodness in the world. We will also meet her in chapter 5 on love and relationship angels.

Though you can call on these particular angels, your home will have its own special angel that will come any time you ask while preparing, serving, or eating a meal. You can use any of the methods I have suggested in the previous chapters to identify your own mealtime and kitchen angel, who tends to wear colours of the harvest.

Angelic crystals for mealtimes and the kitchen
Keep a small dish of any or all of these crystals on a shelf in the kitchen and another on the table where you eat.

To **protect** your home against fire and electrical or gas faults, use green and purple fluorite water crystals and the protective orange carnelian.

To **energise** your plates and mugs with life force and encourage kind and gentle mealtimes, use green jade, blue lace agate, and white calcite, kept on the table and with crockery.

To **promote friendly, lively communication** and overcome food-related issues in adults and food fads in children, use orange carnelian and amber.

Angel mealtime fragrances
Particular herbs may become associated with your kitchen angel. You may notice, for example, that if you add rosemary to a meal you can feel your angel close by, whereas other herbs do not evoke that feeling. Also, your angel may respond to more than one herb, so experiment: add different dried herbs to meals or grow fresh herbs on your kitchen window ledge.

Create blessings for harmonious mealtimes

Blessing the table and the meal before you eat is a powerful but simple way of drawing positive energies to any occasion, festive or informal, and you can also bless each of the rooms in your home to make your home a place of security, peace, and joy.

I have suggested a blessing that can be used for any mealtime occasion. Remember to bless your meals and table, even if you live alone. Though I have focused on blessing an evening or weekend meal, try a quick blessing at breakfast if you or family members have a stressful day ahead.

A blessing need only take two minutes and can be spoken in your mind, if necessary. You will make up the time with added focus in the morning and a sense of well-being in the evening that can overcome tiredness and irritability left over from the day. A blessing can calm the atmosphere if you have a difficult relative coming or colleagues you do not know very well; preparations will be easier and visitors will respond to the harmonious atmosphere.

✣ BLESSING THE OCCASION

1. Before setting the table, stand in the centre of the area in which you will be preparing the food. Hold one of your kitchen crystals between your hands and say, *"May these hands be filled with love and tranquillity. I ask angel of the kitchen and of happy mealtimes (name the angel if known) to help me prepare this meal joyously and with the minimum of strain caused by time restraints."* (You can add any particular stresses you need help with relating to the cooking or food preparation.)

2. Put down the crystal on the nearest surface and picture the angel surrounding you with its rays, giving you energy, enthusiasm, and a sense of calm, even if you are watching the clock. If you really are desperate

for time, then say the blessing while cooking and put the crystal close by.

3. When the meal is ready, light a single white candle or two or three small tea lights in holders in the centre of the table. Say aloud or in your mind, *"I light this flame in love and peace to call the angel of the kitchen and of happy mealtimes (name the angel if known). I ask that this meal may bring joy/tranquillity to the occasion and a fit ending/beginning of the day. I give thanks for ... (add what you feel is right) and ask strength and patience for ..."* (name any issues that may stop you relaxing and enjoying the meal). If you are struggling financially, ask that you may always have enough food and resources.

4. When you carry the food in and everyone is seated, light a second white candle from the first in the centre of the table to transfer the blessings, and move the first candle to another part of the room. Leave both candles burning. Say in your mind or, if appropriate, aloud, *"May blessings and peace, joy and good companionship, kind words and laughter fill this home and this table. Welcome to all who come in friendship and may the blessings of the angels remain with you."*

Sleep Angels

While each household possesses its own home angel, the angels of sleep will visit any individual or family regardless of where they live, if asked to help with insomnia, adult nightmares, children's night terrors, or fears of the dark.

You may first see a sleep angel in a dream, or become aware of his or her presence as you drift off or when you wake in the morning. The sensation is like a very bright light surrounding you that you are aware of, even though your eyes are still closed.

IDA'S ANGEL OF SLEEP

Ida told me that from the time when she was young, she always slept in complete darkness with her door closed. Ida's mother was amazed that she was not afraid like most other children. Ida always answered that she was safe as she had an angel in the corner of her bedroom. Even in adulthood, the angel remains in her bedroom at night, protecting her. Ida believes she also saw the family household angel on Christmas Eve. This tall white angel was flying above the snow-covered ground around the outside of the house.

To discover the identity of the angel who moves close to you at night, use one of the methods already described, such as working with a pendulum (see pages 40–42). Alternatively, use the "Connecting with your sleep angel" ritual on the next page.

Gabriel is the presiding archangel of sleep and dreams and is very protective of children at night. However, call on the mystical archangel **Raziel** if you want an answer to a question in your dreams or a psychic dream.

Carina, a blue angel with a wool cloak, rocks anyone in her arms if they are sad at night.

Duma is an angel of quiet sleep; she is helpful if you have a stressful life and find it hard to fall asleep or suffer from irregular sleep patterns.

Jeduthan is the angel of the evening and of the twilight heavenly choirs, with an indigo halo and wings. He brings peace into your home in the evening and encourages a quiet transition between sleeping and waking.

Memumah is the angel who sends sleep and soothing dreams if you call on him. A misty silvery angel, he will

relieve nightmares and protect against psychic or psycho-
logical attack while you sleep.

Muriel, a healer angel, brings beautiful dreams to those who
are afraid of the dark. She wears pink and lilac and is surrounded by moonbeams.

Natiel is a lilac-winged angel who keeps away harm and
night terrors from children, and helps older people sleep
through the night.

✣ CANDLES, FRAGRANCES, AND CRYSTALS FOR SLEEP

+ *Candles:* Dark blue, purple, indigo, or silver
+ *Fragrances:* Jasmine, myrrh, or rose are the best
+ *Sleep crystals:* Moonstones, creamy shimmering selenite,
  mother-of-pearl, and rose quartz are most effective

Connecting with your sleep angel

The presleep stage is when the barriers of the conscious mind are
least active. Once you have connected with the sleep angel to whom
you most closely relate, this angel will be the one who always comes
to you unless you specifically call another.

1. Have a quiet half an hour before bedtime so that your mind
   can switch to the gentler flow of night-angel energies. Take
   a bath or slow shower using a jasmine, rose, or gentle floral
   bath product and light the bathroom with scented candles (or
   a soft light).

2. About ten minutes before you go to bed, burn jasmine,
   rose, or other gentle floral oil in a safe place so the room is
   fragrant. Incense is too harsh. (Blow out the aromatherapy
   burner candle when you go to bed.)

3. Light an indigo, purple, silver, or blue candle in a safe enclosed glass container in the bedroom and, if you wish, have as background one or two fragrance diffusers, also in a safe place if they use candles.

4. Turn off any lights, then lie in bed with half-closed eyes in the candlelight and hold a sleep crystal (see above). There may be one special crystal that connects with your sleep angel that you can discover through experimentation. Rose quartz is an all-purpose sleep crystal.

5. If this is the first time you have worked with your sleep angel and have not yet discovered its name and characteristics, ask that your angel will appear to you in your dreams.

6. Focus on the main candle and picture its colour filling the room as a soft beautiful mist. Imprint the colour on your mind.

7. Now blow out all candles. Gaze into the darkness and imagine the candle colour is still present, superimposed on the darkness. Picture that colour being surrounded by other sleep angel colours: blue, indigo, purple, and silver, plus pink, green, gold, and white so you create a night rainbow of imagined bands of colour in the room. If you cannot easily do this with your eyes open, close your eyes and imagine the colours forming a rainbow.

8. Breathe softly and picture yourself walking up steps of golden light into mists the same colour as the candle you lit, with the other colours forming the background.

9. See yourself in your mind (with eyes open or closed) in a realm where there are beautiful gardens, forests, waterfalls, flowers, trees, and butterflies. You may smell your sleep angel's subtle fragrance. You will become aware, even if you cannot yet see him or her, that your sleep angel is already with you.

10. Ahead are more steps of light, leading to a realm of rose-pink light. You may feel the soft touch of angel wings. Walk upwards on more steps to realms of green, then gold, and finally white. The white realm is quite misty, but you will see quite clearly your angel of sleep and his or her name may come spontaneously into your mind. You may become aware of wonderful music and feel a sense of lightness as though you could easily float away.

11. As you drift into sleep, allow yourself to feel progressively lighter. Float through the deepening blue sky and the stars. You cannot fall, for your angel is holding your hand and will guide you safely back to bed, having shown you things you need to see and answered any questions.

    Even if you do not at first dream of angels, your dreams will be filled with light and angelic energies.

12. When you wake, open your eyes slowly and you may glimpse or sense your sleep angel and your guardian angel behind the sleep angel, waiting to guide you through the day. If you have not already discovered your sleep angel's name, it should come to you now. It may not be one of the above-named sleep angels, for there are many who guide us at night.

Practise this once a week and within a month, your dreams will be filled with angels and you will visit many different places in dreams, protected always by your sleep guardian.

If you sleep with a partner, you could first try this exercise on an evening when you are alone and then you can in future just light a candle in the bedroom presleep and do the rest with visualisation.

✤ SLEEP ON IT

If any night you have specific questions you need answering or are trying to find a creative solution to a problem, write the question on white paper in green ink, then fold and place it under your pillow. Your night angel will help you find the answer in your dreams or in unmistakable signs during the day ahead.

four

HEALING ANGELS

We all have our own healing angel who is part of our personal angelic life team. This healing angel encourages us towards a healthier lifestyle by reducing cravings for unhealthy foods and stimulants and helping us to relax when life becomes too hectic. Though we cannot always expect miracles, our personal healing angel will help our bodies respond to any conventional or alternative medical intervention if we ask, and speed up the healing process. They may even guide us to find information about a new treatment or remedy. The key is always to ask, as then you are giving your angel permission to intervene.

MARY'S HEALING ANGEL

Mary from New Zealand (see chapter 3, page 46) told me of another angelic encounter. In 1996, she was waiting to be taken to hospital with unbearable abdominal pain. She knew something was seriously wrong and so asked for her healing angel to help, as she had so many things she still wanted to do in life. At that moment, Mary became aware of the presence of a beautiful woman dressed in white with long golden hair. The angel reassured Mary and told her that, although it was cancer, Mary need not be afraid as everything would be fine. Mary says she cannot explain how she could be in so much pain and yet feel suddenly good and peaceful, and she even managed to joke in the hospital. As predicted, Mary did have cancer, but responded well to treatment, thanks to her angel, she believes— and twelve years later, Mary is still cancer-free.

While it is not possible to measure how far belief can trigger our own self-healing system to make treatment more effective, in Mary's case the presence of her angel took away all her fear and gave her the certainty that her treatment would be successful.

Working with Your Healing Angel

Your healing angel is always with you. If you need any medical treatment you may feel, sense, or even see extra hands helping the practitioner. As a bonus, any necessary intervention may seem far smoother and less traumatic than usual, and any unpleasant side- or after-effects appear reduced.

In addition, some people discover that working with healing angels awakens their own natural healing abilities. As you put your hand on the head of a loved one suffering from migraine or rub a child's bruised knee, or even as you touch a distressed friend or colleague sympathetically, your angel will allow healing to flow from you without any training on your part.

Healing angels are the most ethereal and difficult to perceive externally, though they may appear temporarily as shimmering light when you are having a crisis or are ill. On these occasions you may observe sparkles of light in the darkest room.

If you are lucky enough to see your healing angels externally (and not everybody does), they appear as misty colours. You may discern your healing angel as radiating pastel rays from a central point of light and see, circled by the rays, the pale outline of angelic form. Blue, lilac, green, or pink are the most common personal healing angel rays. If you haven't yet encountered your healing angel, the following exercise will help you to do so.

Meeting your healing angel

Even if you are already aware of your healing angel, this is a good way to make an even deeper connection.

1. Sit quietly in your angel place and light a pastel-coloured candle.

2. Burn a fruit-scented or gentle floral-fragranced oil. Hold your crystal sphere between your hands or your pendulum in front of your eyes so the candlelight sparkles in the centre. Look within the crystal and ask your healing angel if he or she will appear to you. You may see a misty form appear within the crystal.

3. If nothing happens, put down the ball or pendulum; having made the connection, close your eyes and the angel should appear in your mind.

4. To discover your angel's name, look again into the sphere or through the pendulum and focus on the light reflected from the candle. A name may come into your mind. If you are uncertain, you can use the letter card and pendulum or the automatic writing method (see pages 25 and 40).

An alternative way to meet your healing angel is to use the mirror technique from chapter 3.

Finding your healing angel's coloured ray

Many people do see healing or sense healing rays in their mind's eye. If you have not had any success finding the colour of your healing angel's ray, try the exercise below using your pendulum and you may even be rewarded by an external shimmering that thereafter accompanies your work and connection with your own healing angel.

Once you know your angel's own healing ray colour and any distinguishing fragrance (this will be very soft but fresh), you can include them in your life and home. Alternatively, visualise the colour surrounding you when you feel anxious or exhausted to fill you with the healing energies of your angels. This can bring, for example, soft pink relief that flows through your body when your back is aching from carrying heavy bags or your eyes are hurting and you cannot take a break from the computer screen. You can direct the healing ray energy through your mind as coloured light towards any part of your body that is troubling you.

1. Hold your pendulum a few centimetres over each of the colours on the chart below and ask your healing angel to show you his or her colour by pulling down over the appropriate segment. The nearer to the left-hand side of the chosen segment the pendulum pulls, the darker and more opaque the

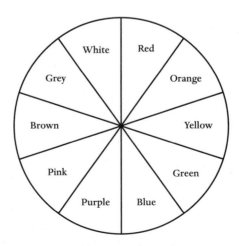

shade will be; the nearer to the right-hand side of the segment, the more pale and transparent it will be.

2. Light the same-coloured candle as the ray to call your healing angel if you are tired, in pain, or ill. Breathe in the candlelight, imagining that the coloured rays are entering and flowing through your body from the crown of your head to your feet. As you exhale, picture any sorrow, pain, blockages, or discomfort flowing out as dark mist through your mouth as you gently exhale. This will be transformed by your healing angel into healing light that will surround you.

Your healing angel's crystal and fragrance

In addition, so you can more easily and readily communicate directly with your healing angel and get faster and more lasting relief from pain or suffering, as well as visualising or burning a candle in the healing ray, use your healing angel's special crystal and fragrance. Discover these by using the following method:

+ Make a circle of any angel crystals you have and pass your pendulum a few centimetres above each one. If you don't have a pendulum or many crystals, don't worry: your healing angel is very adaptable. If you do not own many crystals, he or she will choose your favourite crystal and tune the healing vibrations to that.

+ To discover the angelic fragrance, do the same with a selection of fruit- or floral-scented oils, incense sticks, or real fruit.

+ Alternatively, write the following fragrance names in a circle to make the choice, adding any fragrances you instinctively feel are healing. The most common healing angel fragrances are chamomile, lavender, lily, lilac, myrrh, rose, sandalwood, violet, or any fruit fragrance such as apple or cherry blossom, grapefruit, lemon, lemon balm or lemon verbena, lime, orange or orange blossom, peach, or pear.

• Once you have this information, holding the healing crystal of your angel close to a point of pain or tension will help to direct the healing even more accurately. Once you also know the healing angel fragrance, carry a bottle of the relevant essential oil or floral water and rub it on a pain or on your brow to send healing from your angel throughout your system, wherever you are.

Angel Healing Experiences

Angels often manifest during formal healing sessions. Sometimes the client as well as the therapist becomes aware of an additional healer or healing hands on them.

ANGEL LIGHTS

Johanna in Scotland explained how recently, while she was giving Reiki to a very troubled client, she saw lovely white and blue lights in the room. This has occurred before and these bright sparkling "angel lights," as she calls them, make her feel very happy and protected.

ANGEL WINGS

Anna, who lives in Sweden, explained that after massaging her friend Helena, the friend commented that Anna had really big light-blue wings behind her during the massage. When Anna held her hands on her friend's head, Helena said she had seen a huge light surrounding them.

REIKI ANGEL HELPERS

Jane, who has worked with Reiki for nearly twenty-five years, frequently sees balls of light (orbs) floating around or a shining figure standing or kneeling by the client. Occasionally, clients open their eyes and realise Jane is somewhere else in the room, but they can still feel gentle hands on them.

THE ANGEL WHO HEALED A CHILD

Keith from Wales described how when he was young he was taken to hospital in the Rhondda Valley, desperately ill with meningitis and diphtheria. He became paralysed, and in those days there were no drugs to help. His family was told he was dying.

Keith's grandfather refused to leave the hospital and found a shed on the grounds where he could be alone. He sat in the dark and prayed. Suddenly he saw a light in the roof and a voice asked, *"What's the matter, my son? Why are you crying?"*

Keith's grandfather replied: "My grandson is dying and the doctors can't help him. Can you save him?"

The voice told him that Keith would live, and that he should go back to him and wait. That night, Keith started to get better.

JANE'S GUARDIAN ANGEL

Jane, who lives in north London, suffered a long illness with a severe pancreatic problem. At one point, things were so bad she decided to end it all by taking an overdose, but she could not reach the other side of the room where the morphine was kept. She lay on the floor, exhausted and unable to move. Then she saw an angel step out of the wall and watched herself being led away with the angel's arms around her shoulders. The pain was gone.

She awoke in her bed the next day, had a bath, got dressed, changed the sheets, and did the washing before her son came home from school. Although Jane was still ill, the improvement was incredible.

THE STAR LADY

I was suffering from severe gall bladder pains and one night, after thirty-six hours of sickness and wall-to-wall pain, said in despair, "I know you are there. Please angels, show yourselves to me to give me a single reason to go on."

Through the pain I felt a light pressure on my brow. I looked up and the whole room was filled with golden light. Standing in the corner was a tall woman covered with and radiating gold and white light, with what appeared to be a star over and surrounding her head. She said, *"You had only to ask for help."*

I was aware of warm liquid flowing through me from my brow, through my throat, my heart, and round my stomach, warming and taking away the intense physical pain and the despair. The room remained filled with light for several minutes. The Star Lady faded and the pain was completely eased. I slept for the first time in days.

I have never seen my Star Lady again, though I do see light shimmers out of the corner of my eye when I get really stressed or anxious.

Angels of Healing

As well as your own angel, there are other angels who have been associated throughout time with particular aspects of healing. For just as a general medical practitioner will sometimes refer us to a specialist, so we can ask our healing angel to guide us to the right angel for extra help if we are very worried or an illness does not clear up.

Below is a list of the best-known healing angels and archangels that you can consult for any additional help you need, whether for yourself or a loved one.

You may, with the guidance of your healing angel, know at once which angel to choose. The choice may be obvious because a condition associated with a particular angel or archangel is on the list.

However, if you are uncertain, you can use a pendulum to guide you. Ask your healing angel to help you choose by passing your pendulum slowly down the names to indicate the best angel or angels to assist you. Ask your healing angel to guide the pendulum to vibrate and pull down over the correct angel or to make a positive swing, if you prefer.

Each angel on the list has its own healing crystal and colour ray. If you do not have the right candle colour or crystal, you can substitute those of your personal healing angel. Alternatively, as you hold all your crystals one at a time, ask your healing angel to indicate by a tingling in your palms which will work best with the named angel. White can also be substituted for any angel colour ray.

Your crystal sphere, an amethyst, or clear quartz crystal will also serve as a connecting crystal for any of the named angels or archangels. However, you may wish to purchase the special crystals of those named angels with whom you do a lot of healing work. In time, you can make yourself a set of healing crystals specific to your needs. I have marked with an asterisk those I consider particularly useful.

Use any of the fragrances mentioned above when working with these named healing angels. You may, however, detect their personal fragrance spontaneously.

Anael, archangel of love

DAY: Friday

COLOUR: Green

CRYSTAL: Jade*

DESCRIPTION: Surrounded by rose-pink and green light, with silver wings, often depicted as female

PROMOTES: Healthy growth, regrowth, and regeneration anywhere in the body; recovery or remission from illness

GOOD FOR HEALING: Emotionally rooted and psychosomatic illnesses; anti-tumour; helps with problems with the upper back, rib cage, chest, lymph glands, skin, hands and arms, circulatory system, lungs, breathing difficulties, and related allergic conditions, such as asthma; all matters concerning the heart; frequent coughs, colds, viruses, infections; overemotional outbursts, over-sentimentality, or possessiveness and jealousy

Ariel, archangel of nature

DAY: Sunday

COLOUR: Violet

CRYSTAL: Moss or tree agate*

DESCRIPTION: Violet eyes, long silver hair surrounded by yellow light and a halo of sunshine yellow

PROMOTES: Effectiveness of herbal and homeopathic healing

GOOD FOR HEALING: Animals; the natural world; relieves infections and recurring health problems

Assiel, angel of healing water

DAY: Friday

COLOUR: Pale green

CRYSTAL: Green fluorite*

DESCRIPTION: Misty green and purple with green healing light radiating from his hands

PROMOTES: Healing power of water from sacred springs and wells; empowers angel crystals, spheres, and pendulums with healing light

GOOD FOR HEALING: Bladder problems and bedwetting in children

Bariel, angel of small miracles

DAY: Tuesday

COLOUR: Orange

CRYSTAL: Red jasper*

DESCRIPTION: Colours of sunset

PROMOTES: Helps when a person is not responding to treatment or when the origins of an illness cannot be discovered, such as ME (myalgic encephalomyelitis)

GOOD FOR HEALING: Relieves feelings of being overwhelmed by life, either practically or emotionally

Cassiel, archangel of compassion

DAY: Saturday

COLOUR: Indigo

CRYSTAL: Green aventurine or jet*

DESCRIPTION: Bearded, riding a dragon, and wearing dark robes with indigo flames sparkling from his halo

PROMOTES: Mental balance and ageing gracefully

GOOD FOR HEALING: Pituitary gland, face, brain stem, migraines, balance disturbances; dementia, Alzheimer's, and all problems with ageing and body; mind degeneration or loss of mobility; helps epilepsy and depression

Chamuel or Camael, archangel of courage

DAY: Tuesday

COLOUR: Scarlet

CRYSTAL: Bloodstone or fire agate

DESCRIPTION: Red and green armour or riding a leopard

PROMOTES: Relief for acute conditions and helps in medical emergencies

GOOD FOR HEALING: Blood, bone, and joint disorders; burns, cuts, and wounds; fevers; blood pressure, high and low; problems with anger or aggression

Gabriel, archangel of the moon

DAY: Monday

COLOUR: Silver

CRYSTAL: Moonstone*

DESCRIPTION: Silver or clothed in the blue of the night sky with a robe of stars and a crescent moon for his halo

PROMOTES: Body harmony, self-reliance, confidence; reduces oral cravings

GOOD FOR HEALING: Hormonal imbalance, menstrual and meno-pausal problems; balances all bodily fluids; the reproductive system and fertility, including the production of sperm; the kidneys and bladder; restores harmony with our natural reproductive cycles, biorhythms, and sleep patterns

Maktiel, angel of fruit trees and fruit

DAY: Friday

COLOUR: Lemon yellow or orange

CRYSTAL: Lemon chrysoprase

DESCRIPTION: Has lemon- and orange-coloured wings and halo

PROMOTES: General improvement and maintenance of health

GOOD FOR HEALING: All vitamin and mineral deficiencies; blood sugar problems; eating disorders; skin conditions; digestive disorders, allergies, or food intolerance

Michael, archangel of the sun

DAY: Sunday

COLOUR: Violet, white, or gold

CRYSTAL: Carnelian* or clear quartz*

DESCRIPTION: Golden wings, wearing red and gold armour with sword and shield, carrying the scales of justice or a white banner with a red cross

PROMOTES: General health and long life

GOOD FOR HEALING: Immune system; all neurological conditions; viruses and infections that do not clear; whole body, mind, and spirit healing; brain and personality disorders; good for overcoming feelings of alienation from life or obsession with perfection

Mumiah, angel of medicine and medical research

DAY: Wednesday

COLOUR: White or beeswax

CRYSTAL: Clear quartz crystal or Herkimer diamond

DESCRIPTION: Shining white

PROMOTES: Good response to hospital treatment

GOOD FOR HEALING: Cardiovascular, neurological, or immune problems; promoting healthy bones; giving energy

Raphael, supreme archangel of healing

DAY: Wednesday

COLOUR: Green and/or yellow

CRYSTAL: Citrine*

DESCRIPTION: Surrounded by pure green light and the sparkling yellow of early morning sunshine

PROMOTES: Absolutely any healing need. Assists all healers, physicians, surgeons, and spiritual healers; guides the individual healing angels

GOOD FOR HEALING: Any major health problem; when needing surgery; before and after medical tests and any necessary prolonged chemical or ray treatments; helps digestion, liver, spleen, gall bladder, stomach and small intestine, abdomen, back, muscles, pancreas, adrenal glands, autonomic nerve system, and the metabolism; helps self-confidence; counteracts hyperactivity and workaholic tendencies

Raziel, archangel of mysteries

DAY: Saturday at twilight

COLOUR: Dark green/indigo

CRYSTAL: Apache tear (semitransparent obsidian) or jet

DESCRIPTION: Often seen through mists with grey swirling robes and deep green flares in his halo, or as an outline behind a dark grey semi-transparent curtain

PROMOTES: Guidance of all health workers and caregivers, whether family, friends, or professionals

GOOD FOR HEALING: Pain, especially headaches and migraines; the effects of trauma or abuse; assists the management of lifelong or hereditary conditions

Rehael, angel of health

DAY: Thursday

COLOUR: Any pastel colour

CRYSTAL: Green chrysoprase*

DESCRIPTION: Often seen with a basket of fruit and apple-green robes, wings, and halo

PROMOTES: Health and long life, exercise, fitness, and healthy eating regimes

GOOD FOR HEALING: Flu, colds, coughs, and winter ills, and speeds the recovery from these or any lung or breathing-related conditions; helps to resist harmful technological rays and pollution; assists cell and tissue regeneration and conditions caused by the ageing process

Sachiel, archangel of abundance and the harvest

DAY: Thursday

COLOUR: Sky blue

CRYSTAL: Lapis lazuli* or sodalite*

DESCRIPTION: Wears robes of deep blue and purple, carrying sheaves of corn and baskets of food, with a rich purple and golden halo and blue and purple wings

PROMOTES: Healthy throat and voice

GOOD FOR HEALING: Throat, neck, voice mechanisms, thyroid gland, bronchial passages, jaw, mouth, teeth, the thymus, and the passages running up to the ears; assists with creative blockages; communication difficulties, stuttering, Asperger's syndrome, Tourette's, and autism

Sachluph, angel of flowers

DAY: Monday

COLOUR: Cream

CRYSTAL: Selenite

DESCRIPTION: His wings are made of thousands of white petals

PROMOTES: Treatment involving fragrance, such as aromatherapy, and also flower essences

GOOD FOR HEALING: Sinus problems, hay fever, pollen allergies, and catarrh (excessive mucous discharge associated with colds or congestion)

Uriel, angel of transformation

DAY: Tuesday or Saturday

COLOUR: Ruby red

CRYSTAL: Red jasper or rutilated quartz*

DESCRIPTION: Dressed in rich burnished gold and ruby red with a bright flamelike halo, his open hand holds a flame

PROMOTES: A sense of being connected with life and the ability to make positive connections with others or to move forward

GOOD FOR HEALING: Lower back, hips, legs, knees, and feet; bowels and the large intestine, the anus, prostate gland, and genitals; good for IBS, celiac disease, and constipation; nail splitting; panic attacks or irritability caused by imbalance in the normal flight-or-fight mechanism

Zadkiel, archangel of gentleness

DAY: Thursday

COLOUR: Sky blue

CRYSTAL: Blue celestite*

DESCRIPTION: Surrounded by pale blue light with sky-blue wings

PROMOTES: Therapies such as Reiki, shiatsu, or reflexology

GOOD FOR HEALING: Children and older people and all who are depressed or suffer from fears, addictions, or phobias

Zagveron, angel of salt and purity

Day: Sunday

Colour: White or natural beeswax

Crystal: Clear fluorite

Description: White halo and very slender form

Promotes: Immune system and the speedy healing of wounds

Good for healing: Infections and viruses; arthritis, rheumatism and mobility problems; ulcers; prenatal care, childbirth, and infant care

Heal yourself with angel crystals

Choose the angel you would like to work with, and if possible, work on the chosen angel's special healing day and around dusk or at 10:00 pm, the healing hour. Wednesday is the day of Raphael, the supreme healing angel, and is suitable for any work with your own personal healing angel.

If working with another angel, ask that your own healing angel will assist you to communicate with them. If you are uncertain which angel is best and none of the above seems right, ask your healing angel if they will connect you with the angel energies most suited.

You will also need an angel elixir; prepare this before you begin the exercise by placing any angel crystal in a glass of water for an hour. The water becomes the elixir.

1. Light a candle the colour of your own healing angel or that of the specific named angel or archangel. If you wish, burn an angel fragrance.

2. At the start of the session, to focus on angelic healing, hold the crystal of either your own healing angel or, if you have it, the crystal belonging to the angel or archangel you have chosen. However, you can use your clear quartz crystal sphere, a clear quartz crystal, an amethyst, or a rose quartz as substitutes for absolutely any healing crystal.

3. Relax and state your name and the purpose of the healing.

4. Welcome your healing angel (you may be aware of this presence, and after carrying out a number of healing angel rituals, you may be able to describe this angel in great detail). Welcome any other angels you are working with and ask that they bless and protect the healing.

5. Hold the crystal for a few moments, close your eyes, and picture light entering through your hands. Your fingertips and palms may tingle and you may feel the angels move close.

6. When you feel ready, hold the relevant crystal over the candle flame for a moment or two and ask that the angel(s) fill it with the light of healing. It is good to say the words aloud. Request also that any healing may be for the highest good and with the purest intention.

7. If you are using incense or oil, pass the crystal through the smoke, requesting the help of the angels and naming the purpose of the healing.

8. Hold the empowered crystal a few centimetres above the place on the body representative of the discomfort or close to the centre of the brow for an emotional or spiritual issue.

9. Move the crystal slowly anticlockwise and ask the angel(s) to guide your hand in the ways of healing. You may feel a gentle hand enclosing yours. Picture the crystal drawing out any pain, blockages, infection, fear, addiction, or discomfort, or slowing down any overactivity. You may see rays of the crystal colour but darker, like mist, leaving the crystal and usually moving away upwards or towards any light source.

10. Ask the chosen angel(s) to take away any pain or illness and to bring lasting healing or relief in the way and at the time that will be of most help.

11. The crystal will slow down in its own time, but if you feel your hand and the crystal drawn to another place, allow this to happen.

12. When the crystal finally stops moving, dip it three times into the angel elixir.

13. Then hold the crystal to the candle flame once more and ask the angels that the light of healing may enter to bring renewed strength and enthusiasm. Precisely what you ask to be taken away and given in its place will depend on the nature of the condition.

14. When you feel ready, hold the crystal over the original place on the body from which you drew pain and ask that the angel(s) will bring healing light, blessings, radiance, hope, and energy (you can be specific if you wish, or you may prefer to leave the blessing general).

15. Ask that your hand be guided in the ways of healing. This time, move the crystal clockwise. When you sense the crystal slowing, ask the angels in your mind if there is any other area that needs extra energising and allow your hand to be guided. Hold the crystal there until it stops.

16. Blow out the candle, but leave any fragrance to burn through. Send the extinguished candlelight to yourself or whoever else needs it.

17. Thank the angels for their blessings and place the crystal in the water for a few minutes to cleanse it.

Absent healing with the angels

You can transmit angel healing over great distances to people, animals, or places by using a written name or a photograph, or by putting healing into a gift you intend to give or send to a sick person. As with contact healing, choose the appropriate angel(s) or work with your own healing angel. Gabriel as the messenger archangel and Raphael as the archangel of travel and travellers are particularly appropriate for distance healing.

1. Choose the appropriate candle, incense, and crystal. Set any gift you are sending in front of the candle.

2. Light the candle and, holding the crystal between your cupped hands, ask the healing angel(s) to assist and protect you. State that your healing is for the highest good and with the purest intention, asking that it will be received at the time and in the way most needed. This allows the absent person's healing angel to transmit the healing in the way it can be best used. If you are healing an animal, either directly or as absent healing, you could ask Hariel, the archangel of pets, to help. His candle colour is brown and his crystal jade. You could substitute amethyst as, like jade, is sufficiently gentle for an animal or bird.

3. Name the person, animal, or place to which you are sending healing and specify aloud or in your mind the purpose of the healing.

4. Gently rest the crystal against the centre of your brow and close your eyes. This is the main energy centre through which you receive power from the angels that is transmitted downwards from the cosmos. Picture in your mind the person or animal you are healing as strong and healthy again, or the target place peaceful and all people there having everything they need. Say, *"May it be so with the blessings of the angels."*

5. Hold the crystal outstretched in your hands so the candlelight is reflected in it.

6. Gaze into the crystal (even if is opaque) and project (push mentally) into the crystal the image of the person or animal happy and healthy, or the place restored to wholeness and harmony.

7. When you sense the crystal filled with the angelic light, say aloud or in your mind, *"I send the healing light of the angels to ..."* (name the person or place) so that (state in your own words the ideal outcome), then say, *"I call the blessings of the angels as I work in perfect love and perfect trust."*

8. Imagine beams of light from the crystal floating towards the recipient and surrounding him, her, or with the angel healing. Hold the crystal until you sense the energies and light fading and you know the crystal has done its work.

9. Extinguish the candle and thank the angels. Wash the crystal under running water and leave it to dry naturally. Repeat the ritual whenever you feel it is necessary.

Leave the empowered angel crystal on top of the photograph or written name overnight in your angel place for extra power.

five

LOVE AND RELATIONSHIP ANGELS

B ecause angels want us to be happy, they naturally encourage good relationships. If you ask the angels of love (see page 90 for a list) and your guardian angel, they will help you to find the right person, encourage happy, faithful relationships, and strengthen a partnership in times of difficulty.

Of course, you cannot expect angels to act as a dating agency with a 100 percent success rate. Everyone has free will, and even a seemingly ideal love match may be unsuccessful because of the other person's choice. However, even in difficult circumstances, angelic intervention can cut through barriers and obstacles in love to strengthen mind-to-mind connection with a hesitant lover or build bridges where there is conflict.

I have directed a number of people to light a green candle on a Friday for Anael, archangel of love, and to drop a shredded rose petal into the flame, asking for an inattentive or temporarily distracted lover to make contact (always with the proviso *"if it is right to be"*). Even if the lover chooses not to respond, usually after such a request the right person does come along within three months.

WENDELA'S CUPID ANGEL

Wendela, who lives in Sweden, had been in love with her friend Erik for three years. She was worried he was not the right one and he was shy about declaring his love for her.

They were playing darts in a pub one night when an old man seemed to appear out of nowhere. He told Wendela that very soon her wishes would finally come true and that he could see there was a very special lasting love between her and Erik. Then the old man told Erik that he was holding the arrows of love. Erik threw the dart and scored a bull's-eye, the first one that night. Suddenly the man disappeared and in a second was across the other side of the room, smiling at Wendela. Then he totally vanished. Wendela and Erik are sure the old man was their lucky love angel that brought them together in a time of doubt. Scoring the bull's-eye was a way the more practical Erik could understand the message.

As I said earlier in the book, angels will often appear in a form that is appropriate to the setting, so if anyone else does see them, no one will freak out. Arrows of love go back to the Roman god Cupid, son of Venus, with his bow and love darts. Cupid has become in Christianised folk tradition the angel who brings love, especially to young lovers, and still shoots his silvery darts to awaken a love that is uncertain.

Angels and Twin Souls

It was Plato, the ancient Greek philosopher, who first mentioned the idea of a twin soul. Some may be lucky enough to find their twin soul the first time they fall deeply in love. But for many, it takes years of searching until meeting someone totally unexpectedly, and instantly feeling as though they've encountered that person before. The other person, too, may recognise you as the missing piece in their life. In a short time, you both feel as if you have known each other forever, discovering uncannily similar beliefs, life events, and interests together and with a sense you have come home at last.

You can ask your guardian angel or Mihael, the angel of twin souls, to assist you in finding your "other half." If successful, this new intense relationship will be lasting and grow deeper every day. In other cases, the twin souls may already be involved with other people and have families they cannot leave or circumstances that make it hard for them to be together. However, there may be a time in the future when it is right for you both to unite. Occasionally, your angel may bring someone entirely new in soul terms into your life so you can develop parts of yourself that will enable you to love deeply and fulfil parts of your destiny you have as yet not explored.

MARIA'S TWIN SOUL ANGEL

Maria met her twin soul, Tony, while both were unhappily married to other people. In fact, Tony was the best childhood friend of Maria's husband, Pete. Both Maria and Tony were gifted amateur artists who independently dreamed of moving to France and setting up a small gallery. But neither of their respective partners encouraged their talents.

Maria planned a landscape painting weekend to the Lake District. It seemed natural when Tony suggested driving her and sharing the petrol. Neither of their spouses had any problem with this, as both were workaholics and used the weekend to catch up in their respective offices.

At first Maria was very shy at being alone with Tony, but they soon discovered many similarities and before long were finishing each other's sentences. By the end of the weekend they realised they were twin souls. Being honest people, they both resisted the physical attraction and took care not to be alone in the future.

Some time later, Maria's marriage broke up and she lost touch with Tony. Then one day she heard through Pete's mother that Tony had been abroad but was coming home as his marriage had ended. Maria asked her guardian angel and the archangel Anael to make Tony find her, as she did not know if he had someone else.

Within a week, Maria got an e-mail from Tony, directed via Pete's mother to ask if she had some old school photographs of Pete and his classmates as Tony was trying to organise a class reunion. Maria replied to the mail. The class reunion never happened but Maria and Tony are now together. As with so many apparent coincidences that move events along, Maria would never have had the courage to contact Tony when she was divorced, nor would she have ever asked her ex-mother-in-law for his e-mail address, had it not been for the reunion.

SENDING LOVE VIA THE ANGELS

There is a big overlap in the roles of angels who rule romantic love and relationships and those who help when any relationship goes wrong. I have listed the most significant love angels alphabetically below, so you can call on the right angel for your need. You can find others who assist in all matters of love in the list of 250 angels at the back of the book (see page 227).

+ If you are in a hurry, all you need do is light the appropriate coloured candle, call the chosen love angel, and name your lover, desired lover, or *"someone who would make me happy."* Speak into the flame any words of love or reconciliation you would wish to say, as if the person were present and you were able to speak from your heart. The angel will carry your message. (Bear in mind, though, that there is no guarantee of its effect because of the other person's free will to reject even a love that would be perfect.)

+ At the moment you blow out the candle, in your mind send the light to your lover or to someone as yet unknown to pick up the signal.

+ You could wear the angel's gem, crystal, or metal as jewellery, wear their fragrance as perfume or substitute your favourite perfume, and wear the angelic colour on a date or special occasion in your relationship.

+ Light the angel love candle as often as you wish for a few minutes, especially on the angel's own day, and put your jewellery next to the lit candle to empower it.

+ If you are not in a hurry, use the love candle to light an incense stick in the angel's fragrance. Using the incense stick smoke as a pen, write your lover's name and a few words of love in the air and ask the angel to transmit what you have imprinted on the aether (spiritual space.)

+ For family reconciliation or to send love to an absent family member, you could light the candle in your heart of the home angel centre (see "The angelic heart of your home" in chapter 3, page 50).

Love and relationship angels

ADRIEL

DESCRIPTION AND ROLES: An angel of the week after the full moon. Brings spiritual depths to lovemaking; helps in any difficult times in marriage or long-term relationship. Call on him to keep a partner from straying. Silver and slightly misty in appearance.

SPECIAL DAY: Monday or the week after the full moon

COLOUR (FOR CANDLE, CLOTHING, JEWELLERY, ETC.): Light blue

FRAGRANCE: Neroli or orange

CRYSTALS / GEMS / METALS: Sapphire or any blue stone

ATLIEL

DESCRIPTION AND ROLES: Angel of the full moon. Helps fertility or to bring a child into your life by adoption or surrogacy; for increasing or reviving passion in any relationship. Silver and gold robes.

SPECIAL DAY: Monday or the day of the full moon

COLOURS (FOR CANDLE, CLOTHING, JEWELLERY, ETC.): Silver for fertility, red for passion

FRAGRANCES: Jasmine or poppy

CRYSTALS / GEMS / METALS: Silver, amber, or moonstone for fertility; red jasper, carnelians, or garnets for passion

ANAEL, ANIEL, OR HANIEL

DESCRIPTION AND ROLES: Archangel of love, fertility and fidelity. Calls and keeps love in your life; good for mending quarrels and estrangement, and for bringing stepfamilies together. Surrounded by rose-pink and green light and silver wings.

SPECIAL DAY: Friday

COLOURS (FOR CANDLE, CLOTHING, JEWELLERY, ETC.): Rich green or pink

FRAGRANCE: Rose and fresh or dried rose petals

CRYSTALS / GEMS / METALS: Jade or rose quartz, copper

DIRACHIEL

DESCRIPTION AND ROLES: An early waxing moon angel who will call new love and friendship; helps with any love that must be kept secret and love that faces obstacles. Has a crescent moon halo.

SPECIAL DAY: Monday

COLOUR (FOR CANDLE, CLOTHING, JEWELLERY, ETC.): Silver

FRAGRANCE: Lemon

CRYSTALS / GEMS / METALS: Lemon chrysoprase or selenite

DONQUEL

DESCRIPTION AND ROLES: The angel of finding true love. A twin soul angel, good for increasing or reviving passion. Sparkling scarlet wings.

SPECIAL DAY: Tuesday

COLOUR (FOR CANDLE, CLOTHING, JEWELLERY, ETC.): Red

FRAGRANCES: Cinnamon or ginger

CRYSTALS / GEMS / METALS: Red jasper or gold

ERGEDIEL

DESCRIPTION AND ROLES: Angel of the day before the full moon. For increased commitment in love; for marriage or any permanent commitment. An angel with shimmering silver and gold robes.

SPECIAL DAY: Monday or the night before the full moon

COLOUR (FOR CANDLE, CLOTHING, JEWELLERY, ETC.): White

FRAGRANCES: Lemon grass or jasmine

CRYSTALS / GEMS / METALS: Moonstone or rainbow moonstone

GELIEL

DESCRIPTION AND ROLES: An angel of the last quarter of the waning moon. Brings reconciliation between lovers and in families. Softly shimmers silver and gold from her wings and halo.

SPECIAL DAY: Monday or any time when the moon is almost gone from the sky

COLOUR (FOR CANDLE, CLOTHING, JEWELLERY, ETC.): Pink

FRAGRANCES: Lavender or rose

CRYSTALS / GEMS / METALS: Moonstone or silver

Iris

DESCRIPTION AND ROLES: Angel of the rainbow. Comforts those who have lost loved ones, especially a love partner, whether in death or desertion; will give strength to leave a hopeless situation; blesses love in later life and helps new trust grow. Rainbow wings.

SPECIAL DAY: Saturday

COLOURS (FOR CANDLE, CLOTHING, JEWELLERY, ETC.): Lilac or rainbow stripes

FRAGRANCE: Lilac

CRYSTALS / GEMS / METALS: Rainbow varieties of moonstone, obsidian, quartz, or opal

Mihael

DESCRIPTION AND ROLES: Angel of lasting love, of twin souls and fidelity. Also the angel of self-love. Deep green wings and halo.

SPECIAL DAY: Thursday

COLOUR (FOR CANDLE, CLOTHING, JEWELLERY, ETC.): Blue

FRAGRANCE: Sandalwood

CRYSTALS / GEMS / METALS: Lapis lazuli or emerald

Pahaliah

DESCRIPTION AND ROLES: Angel of faith and trust. Will help when you need to keep faith with difficult people or to trust after betrayal. Halo of pale lilac and wings of a deeper purple.

SPECIAL DAY: Sunday

COLOURS (FOR CANDLE, CLOTHING, JEWELLERY, ETC.): White or cream

FRAGRANCE: Chamomile

CRYSTALS / GEMS / METALS: Angelite or pewter

RACHIEL

DESCRIPTION AND ROLES: Angel of romance and family loyalties. Attracts new love to you or deepens commitment. Wings and halo of deep pink.

SPECIAL DAY: Friday

COLOUR (FOR CANDLE, CLOTHING, JEWELLERY, ETC.): Pink

FRAGRANCE: Mimosa

CRYSTALS / GEMS / METALS: Any pink crystal or copper

REQUIEL

DESCRIPTION AND ROLES: Angel of the late waning moon. For letting go of a destructive relationship or one that has run its course. Very misty in appearance.

SPECIAL DAY: Monday

COLOURS (FOR CANDLE, CLOTHING, JEWELLERY, ETC.): Indigo or deep purple

FRAGRANCE: Myrrh

CRYSTALS / GEMS / METALS: Opal or celestite

SEREDA

DESCRIPTION AND ROLES: A motherly angel. Will mend any quarrels or coldness among loved ones and bring together stepfamilies or people with very different backgrounds or from different generations. Soft apricot-coloured wings.

SPECIAL DAY: Friday

COLOUR (FOR CANDLE, CLOTHING, JEWELLERY, ETC.): Golden brown

FRAGRANCES: Patchouli or carnation

CRYSTALS / GEMS / METALS: Golden tiger's eye or amber

SHEKINAH

DESCRIPTION AND ROLES: Blesses women whenever they make love to
   their life partner or to someone they love and respect. Believed to
   be present at all marriages or when a couple informally promise
   commitment to each other. A bright white angel.

SPECIAL DAY: Friday

COLOURS (FOR CANDLE, CLOTHING, JEWELLERY, ETC.): White or green

FRAGRANCES: Lavender or orange blossom (neroli)

CRYSTALS / GEMS / METALS: Jade, silver, or gold

TAGRIEL

DESCRIPTION AND ROLES: Angel of the waning crescent moon. Helps
   us to finally say goodbye to a relationship that is dead, or which
   we hold on to out of habit or fears of being alone. Almost transparent in appearance.

SPECIAL DAY: Monday or the end of the moon period

COLOUR (FOR CANDLE, CLOTHING, JEWELLERY, ETC.): Indigo

FRAGRANCE: Myrrh

CRYSTALS / GEMS / METALS: Jet or black apache tear

Angel Altars of Love and Fidelity

The most powerful way to attract or keep faithful love or to mend a
relationship is to set up a love angel altar in your special angel place,
or in a separate place if you are going to use it regularly.

   You cannot have too many angel places around your home; the
energies will bounce as light from one place to another, enhancing
the overall love and happiness vibes flowing throughout your home.
You may find it helpful to carry out simple love angel rituals, repetitive words and actions, over a period of weeks or months in your
love angel place. These rituals build up love energies in your life so
you can more easily attract or increase existing love. They can even
be used to ease ties that may be deep between you and a loved one
but now are causing pain, so you know that you must part. There-

fore, I have focused mainly on rituals as the best way of working with love angels.

By lighting the right coloured candles and making empowering statements about the desired state of love, you can harness the natural power we all possess to draw what it is we most desire to us and maintain it.

Even if you only have a few minutes a day, once you have gathered together the crystals, candles, and symbols of your love purpose, you can follow a simple daily ritual and a slightly longer one on the angel's special day.

Every time you work with your love altar, you increase its power. You can carry one of the empowered crystals or symbols whenever you are seeking to attract love. You can also bathe in the fragrance of the particular angel, having left the bath product on the altar for a few hours, and even endow your favourite perfume with angelic power by setting it in the candlelight every time you light your love-altar candle.

Creating a love altar

If you do not have a particular candle or crystal colour, choose a pink candle or crystal for love and reconciliation, green or blue for fidelity, red for passion, and purple for letting go. Rose and lavender are multipurpose fragrances for any love issues or needs.

Your focal angel is Anael.

YOU WILL NEED:

+ A pink cloth
+ A bowl of small rose quartz crystals (or pink glass nuggets)
+ Twin matching pink candles in identical candleholders
+ Rose, lavender, or jasmine incense sticks and a holder
+ A picture of idealised lovers, perhaps a downloaded image of an old painting from the Internet, but choose lovers whose relationship ends happily

- If you already know the person and you have a photograph, plus a picture of yourself, set them side by side so the images touch. You can also write your names in red ink on white paper.
- A small bottle (not spray) of your favourite fragrance

A LOVE ALTAR RITUAL

1. Light the candles, the second from the first, and say, "I (name) call on loving Anael to bring me new love and call into my life the person who will make me happy and I him/ her." If there is someone you especially like you can adapt the words and name the person, but add "or the person who will make me happy" (in case the one you desire is not right for you).

2. Make a heart shape to enclose the picture(s) or the names with the rose quartz crystals or nuggets in the centre of the altar (you can leave this permanently once set up).

3. Now light an incense stick from each candle in turn and write in the air over the candle, using the incense stick like a pen: "Come love and find me, come love and stay with me, throughout eternity."

4. Blow out the candles, saying, "Love find me," and leave the incense to burn through. You can reuse the candles until they will no longer light.

5. If you are going out for the evening, take your fragrance bottle and put a drop on each of your inner wrist points that are connected to your heart chakra energy centre and say, "I open my heart to the love that is right for me."

Creating a commitment and fidelity altar

A commitment and fidelity altar will help to deepen the love if it is the right one for you. Thereafter you could keep a mini marriage or commitment altar to preserve love and faithfulness and carry out a blessing ritual, based on the one below, on significant anniversaries. It also maintains connections if you hit a difficult patch or one of you must live away for a while.

Your focal angel is Shekinah.

You will need:

+ A green cloth
+ Two identical jade crystals
+ Matching rich green or white candles in identical holders
+ A single red rose in a vase to symbolise the unity of love. You may only wish to add this on anniversaries. If your partner gives you flowers, you could substitute these.
+ Any entwined figure statue, two identical jade animals, two identical glass butterflies or, in feng shui style, two mandarin duck models side by side facing the same way.
+ Two rings, either thin gold or silver ones, or two jade rings on a small pink silk or velvet square. Or, use your commitment or wedding rings if doing the following ritual together with your partner. The ritual is also a good occasion to bless and dedicate commitment rings as you ask for Shekinah's blessings; you could sprinkle them with dried lavender heads or anoint them with three drops of lavender oil, her special fragrance.

❧ A COMMITMENT RITUAL

1. Light the candles, lighting one from the other, and name yourself and your partner.

2. Ask both your guardian angels and Shekinah to keep you united. You can adapt the words according to what is on your mind; if, for example, you or your partner must be away for a while or an interfering relative is coming to stay.

3. Pass the two rings over each candle flame in turn, saying, *"Round and 'round the ring of truth, love in age and love in youth, love in sickness and in health, love in hardship, love in wealth. This I ask in love and with good intentions."*

4. Blow out the candles one after the other and leave all in the hands of Shekinah.

5. If doing this ritual with your partner, after you have dedicated the rings, rather than blowing out the two green candles, light a third, larger green candle from the two separate ones. As you do so, each of you can pledge love and commitment and say what you offer the other. You would then blow out the separate candles, saying, *"Now we two shall be one, are one as long as the waters of the earth flow and the sun shines. We ask Shekinah to bless our home whenever we light a candle in the name of love."*

6. Leave the large candle to burn through.

Trouble in Paradise—Relationship and Family Angels

All too often, pressures of work, money troubles, interference from outsiders, and a multitude of other reasons cause relationship problems and family estrangements. You can call on reconciliation angels as well as your household angel to help resolve family crises and coldness, as well as to restore lost love or call back a lover who has left you but with whom there are still deep feelings. This time, rather than setting up an altar, you can carry out a private daily ritual in your special angel place for reconciliation. Light a candle in the colour of one of the reconciliation angels such as Geliel (pink) and ask for your love to return. You then speak some words of love, as though your partner was present, before blowing out the candle. You may need to do this several times, especially if a partner has been unfaithful but you believe the relationship can survive with the help of the angels.

Healing relationships or restoring a lost love

You can call on Geliel, an angel of the last quarter of the waning moon, for the moon rules the waters of the earth, especially the tides, and is associated with the return of love. This is based on an old sea ritual where the wives of sailors would take from the sea a bottle of water as their lovers' ships sailed out and then, when the ship was expected back, poured the water back in the sea, saying, *"Lady Mother of the Sea, I return what is yours, return mine to me."*

Gradually the ritual was adapted for restoring a person after all love partings and Geliel, the gentle moon angel, was a natural choice to soften anger and call back fidelity, affection, and love. It works equally well for healing family quarrels or bitterness.

✵ AN ANGEL RECONCILIATION RITUAL

1. This is an outdoor ritual. Go to a place where you can easily half fill a small jug of water, for example from a pool, a fountain, a large water feature or best of all, the sea. If really stuck, half fill a washbasin and put in the plug and afterwards drain it away with words of love.

2. As you take the water in your jug, say, *"I ask gentle Geliel to take away all bitterness, coldness, and anger and to bring love/my love back."* (Adapt the words to fit the situation and person from whom you are estranged.)

3. Hold the jug between your hands and speak the words you would like to say if only the other person would listen. Then ask Geliel to carry the words to where they will be heard.

4. Now speak the age-old words to call love back: *"Kind Geliel, moon angel, who rules the waters and calls back whoever is lost or has turned away from me, I return these waters to their source. Return I ask, Geliel, my love to me."*

5. Pour the water back into its source.

Creating angel love rituals

Though the rituals I have suggested work well because they are rooted in tradition, you can create your own angel love rites, using the angels listed above and their associated fragrances and so on. Be as creative as you wish; for example, using photographs as a focus for love angel blessings or writing a loved one's name on paper or in incense smoke over an angelic love crystal. You could also light a beeswax candle and etch your two names in a circle of melted wax, enclosed by an etched heart shape. These you could keep on your love altar or hide in your lover's home.

Alternatively, to attract love or increase commitment, you could carry with you all day an angel love crystal on which you have softly breathed three times at first light, asking the appropriate angel to bring you the love of the person or the commitment you desire.

You could carry the same love angel crystal with you on dates or put it by the computer or phone while talking, sending a text message, or even chatting online with a prospective lover or the person you would like to know better.

To call love back, whisper softly into a reconciliation angel crystal, the words the estranged person rejects, then bury the crystal along with a few seeds beneath a thriving tree, or cast it into flowing water with white petals at twilight, asking an angel of reconciliation to bring peace.

ENDING LOVE WITH GENTLENESS

Finally, Requiel is the angel of kind partings.

+ To end love, you could speak your regrets and, if you have any residual anger, let it go (but speak softly) at 10:00 PM while holding the crystal of the angel of partings. Requiel crystals are blue celestite and opal, but you can choose a rough-cut and inexpensive opal. If possible, end with words of forgiveness or acceptance. Breathe your three last words softly on the crystal three times, and then bury it where nothing grows. Ask Requiel to take the sad or bitter feelings away to leave you free.

+ Alternatively, hold a long piece of dark purple or indigo sewing thread in the flame of an indigo candle, so the middle of the thread breaks as it burns. Say, "*I*

ask kindly Requiel to cut the ties that hold me to ..." (name
the person from whom you wish or need to part). Put
the two ends of the burned thread in a small bowl of
soil and again bury them where nothing grows. This
can be helpful if you are in a destructive relationship
and have lost the will to leave, but know you must to
survive. It also helps if you did not want the parting
but the other person is adamant.

• You could also reverse the commitment ritual and
light a large, dark purple Requiel candle and then,
from it, light two smaller indigo or dark purple candles, naming one for yourself and one for the other
person. Say, *"We now are two again and must go our
separate ways in peace and blessings. We ask that gentle
Requiel take us along new paths to fulfilment and love when
the time is right."*

• Extinguish the large candle and the candle repre-
senting the other person, sending words of love or
forgiveness if you can, or if not, saying, *"Go in peace
and blessings."* Leave your candle to burn through.

Angels who watch over relationships

Angels protect all family relationships, not just romantic ones. You
can ask Anael, Shekinah, or any of the love angels who seem appropriate to care for your loved ones when they are in distress or danger
and to bring peace or reconciliation in family quarrels. The following
cases are ways angels have intervened in family crises or dilemmas.

A GRANDMOTHER'S LOVE
BRINGS DIVINE PROTECTION

Dalma, who lives in Bristol, recalled how one Thursday evening at about 7:45 PM, she knew her fifteen-year-old grandson, Lee, was in danger. She opened her Bible and saw the phrase, *"Snatch them from the fire."* She was afraid Lee was trapped in a fire and so prayed over and over again, *"Snatch Lee from the fire."* At last she felt the danger had passed.

The next day, Lee was very upset when he visited his grandmother and told her that the previous evening he had been about to get into a stolen car full of boys. As Lee was climbing into the back seat, a bigger boy had pushed him aside. At 8:00 PM, the car went out of control and crashed on a suspension bridge and went into the water. All the boys in the car were killed. Lee had seen the accident on the morning news.

THE ANGEL WHO BROUGHT
PEACE TO A WARRING FAMILY

Julie, who lives in Hertfordshire, said that she had experienced a very abusive childhood, yet in adulthood still tried (and failed) to be what her parents wanted. Now in her late thirties, Julie finally had the courage to write a letter saying she no longer wanted contact with her parents.

After she mailed the letter, Julie sat in the middle of a field, terrified of the outcome, saying, "Angels, please help me," over and over. A voice spoke behind Julie, saying, *"What is it you want?"* Julie turned and just caught out of the corner of her eye a tall, brightly lit figure. As she turned, the light was gone. The voice asked again what it was she wanted, and Julie replied to be left alone by her family and not be bullied or harassed anymore. The answer was, *"As you will."* As Julie turned again, the edges of the light figure had returned. Julie says she knew she had seen an angel and she practically floated home.

The next day, her fear had returned. However, later in the day her father sent a text; the message simply said, "As you will." That was not the answer to everything, but it helped to set Julie free.

As my Star Lady said to me when I was in pain, you have only to ask the angels. They cannot make uncaring lovers or relatives into saints, but they can help us to move on and find the love we all deserve.

six

ANGELS AT WORK

Each workplace has an angelic guardian who is easy to connect with, and once you have made that link, you will find that your career runs more smoothly. This angel will also help prevent minor accidents, spats with colleagues, and careless mistakes. Often misty in appearance, the workplace guardian may be mistaken for a ghost. This angel tends to be very attached to the building, and even new premises (perhaps to the original land). Most times, you do not learn their name because workplace guardian angels are more attached to the place than the people, though a name may come into your mind.

If you have ever worked alone outside regular hours, you may have been aware of a benign protective presence or energy force. You may catch out of the corner of your eye a glimpse of a shining angelic outline as you are collecting things from a dark storeroom, or the angel may be standing behind you protectively if someone is being bullying or confrontational.

If you work from home, are raising a family, or caring for a relative, your household angel (see chapter 3) will also be the guardian of your workplace.

THE ANGEL IN THE STOREROOM

Paul worked as the head pharmacist at a large drugstore. He had heard stories about the storeroom ghost, but did not believe in such things. One evening after closing time, Paul went up to the storeroom to collect some medicines that had been delivered earlier in crates. As he reached up to lift the top crate, he dislodged all the others. At that moment—as if in slow motion—Paul became aware of being gently but urgently lifted out of the way and landing safely on the other side of the room. All he saw was a flash of dazzling white light.

When Paul reported the careless stacking of the crates the next day and related how he could have been badly hurt (he did not mention being apparently carried out of the way), everyone laughed and said it was the storeroom ghost.

Connecting with Your Workplace Angel

Workplace angels can be welcomed by placing a large crystal, such as an unpolished blue celestite or an amethyst pyramid, in your workspace as a mini altar, along with a growing fragrant flower or plant. The workplace angel will attract abundance to a company and those who work there as long as there is an honest work ethic. If you do work for a ruthless company with rigid targets and a lot of pressure, your angel crystal will create an oasis of tranquillity for you.

+ Sit for two minutes at the beginning and end of work holding your crystal to create a barrier against stress around you. Wash it weekly under running water or set it on the soil of the plant.

+ Go in early when the building is quiet or stay late one evening and you may sense a gentle rustling almost like a mouse.

+ Look towards the darkest area through half-closed eyes (with minimum lighting) and you may see or sense a floating mist. Relax your eyes and there may be a blurry outline. Don't feel spooked—feel blessed.

+ Hold the crystal and ask if the angel of the workplace will give you a sign of its presence and assist you in your work.

+ In pre-Christian times when these angels were thought of as land guardians, offerings of food would be made. If you keep your plant watered and healthy, and plant it in earth near the building when it wilts, that will serve as an offering.

+ If you own the company, manage a department, or work from home, explain in your mind or out loud any changes that are taking place in the workplace as it will help them go far more smoothly.

+ Explain to the workplace angel why anyone is leaving and who is replacing them. You may wish to do this even if you are an employee, as it will benefit everyone. If you start a new job, try to introduce yourself to the workplace angel and keep a link with the benign energies of your former workplace angel by setting your crystal in your new workspace. However, buy a new plant and leave the old one.

+ Should a business problem arise, tell the angel about it—whether you are the owner or employee—before you go home and perhaps set a tiny angel crystal on a window ledge near where you work, where it can catch the light (angels love jade or moss agate). Then forget your worry. By the next morning an answer will come—either through your own efforts or an unexpected intervention.

You may find other workers start to bring in crystals and plants and the atmosphere will become harmonious as a result. You can adapt the above suggestions if you use a special area or room at home for work. A titanium aura crystal on your home workbench or desk will greatly improve productivity and help protect against computer problems.

Career Angels

As well as a workplace guardian angel, each job has an angelic energy associated with it. You may have been drawn to a particular career from childhood or perhaps a series of coincidences led you to your present position. However, if you want a change, you should still work with your current career angel to maximise existing opportunities. At the same time, you can ask the angel of your chosen career to guide you towards opportunities to train or practise your gifts in a new direction.

If a particular angel for your career is not listed on pages 109–118, you can call upon the angel of your job title, such as asking the assistance of the angel of traditional crafts if, for example, you wanted to start a business making traditional dream catchers.

How to connect with a chosen career angel

You do not need to use any special colours or tools. Find a small token symbolising your career or desired job to act as a lucky talisman. For instance, you could choose a St. Christopher medallion to wear if you wanted to be a travel representative, to link you with the archangel Raphael or the angel Ambriel, the patrons of travel. The more you wear or carry it, the more your angel or angels will fill it and you with confidence.

You could also choose what is called in spiritual traditions a "power tool" connected with your job. Anything that helps you fulfil a task is a power tool; for example, it could be a removable jump drive for your laptop. Like the St. Christopher medallion, you could hold the power tool between your hands to empower it and yourself. At the same time, you would call on your patron angel or angels and make a particular request for help, or create a mantra consisting of a few relevant words in your mind. If you work in an office or in accountancy, you might call on the angel Daniel as you held a favourite pen and recite in your mind over and over, *"The angel Daniel brings order out of chaos."* Do this whenever you become stressed if there are too many demands on your attention. In time, just by touching your power tool or symbol, the angelic power will flow through you.

I have listed two angels for each career. The first is the more powerful archangel for a major boost of energy, defence, or determination. The second is the ruling angel who can be called upon every day for any matter, even if it seems trivial. If something is important to you, the angel will hear and assist. In the case of a major event like a promotion interview or a takeover, you could call on both the archangel and angel, using the power tool or symbol to focus.

THE ARCHANGELS AND ANGELS OF CAREER

Accountants, auditors, tax officials, financial planners
Ruling archangel: METATRON
Subsidiary angel: DANIEL

Actors, comedians, stage and film performers of all kinds
Ruling archangel: ZADKIEL
Subsidiary angel: OREUS

Administrators, local government and civil service employees
Ruling archangel: MICHAEL
Subsidiary angel: YERATEL

Advertising and publicity workers; conference, wedding, and event planners
Ruling archangel: GABRIEL AND JOPHIEL
Subsidiary angel: VEHUEL OR JEHUEL

Anesthetists, radiographers, and occupational therapists
Ruling archangel: AZRAEL
Subsidiary angel: MURIEL

Artists, sculptors, and graphic designers
Ruling archangel: ZADKIEL
Subsidiary angel: HAEL

Astronomers, astrologers, and meteorologists
Ruling archangel: RAZIEL
Subsidiary angels: JEHUDIEL AND KAKABEL

Bakers, cooks, and chefs
Ruling archangel: JOPHIEL
Subsidiary angel: SEREDA

Bankers and insurance workers
Ruling archangel: SACHIEL
Subsidiary angel: SITAEL

Beauticians and make-up artists
Ruling archangel: ANAEL
Subsidiary angel: ASMODEL

Builders and construction engineers
Ruling archangel: MICHAEL
Subsidiary angel: HUMIEL

Call centre staff, customer services staff
Ruling archangels: RAPHAEL AND ANAEL
Subsidiary angel: GELIEL

Care workers of the elderly
Ruling archangel: CASSIEL
Subsidiary angel: IRIS

Car mechanics, garage personnel
Ruling archangel: MICHAEL
Subsidiary angel: ABDIEL

Clairvoyant, mediums, and all psychics
Ruling archangel: RAZIEL
Subsidiary angel: NITHAIAH

Communications: telecommunications, mobile phone sales people, and postal workers
Ruling archangel: GABRIEL
Subsidiary angel: JEHOEL

Computer programmers, software manufacturers, and computer and antivirus engineers
Ruling archangel: RAPHAEL
Subsidiary angel: LAUVIAH

Counsellors, life coaches, social workers, and psychotherapists
Ruling archangel: ANAEL
Subsidiary angel: KABSHIEL OR IRIS

Dancers, choreographers
Ruling archangel: ANAEL
Subsidiary angel: YAHRIEL

Dieticians, nutritionists, and all connected with food, including restaurant staff
Ruling archangel: GABRIEL
Subsidiary angel: ISDA

Disability workers and teachers; all workers who are blind or partially sighted
Ruling archangels: RAPHAEL AND METATRON (FOR CHILDREN WITH LEARNING DISABILITIES)
Subsidiary angel: NANAEL

Doctors, family practitioners, nurses, and health professionals
Ruling archangel: RAPHAEL
Subsidiary angel: MUMIAH

Drivers such as truck, bus, train, and taxi drivers; chauffeurs and driving instructors

Ruling archangel: MICHAEL

Subsidiary angel: ELEMIAH

Electricians, gas workers, and all who sell electrical or gas appliances, or technological goods

Ruling archangel: URIEL

Subsidiary angel: ORMAZD

Employers and executives

Ruling archangel: SACHIEL

Subsidiary angel: RADUERIEL

Environmentalists and forestry workers; carpenters

Ruling archangel: ARIEL

Subsidiary angel: ZUPHLAS

Examiners, testers, and assessors of all kind

Ruling archangel: SAMAEL

Subsidiary angel: HAMALIEL

Explosives experts, gunsmiths, security officers, and defence experts

Ruling archangel: CAMAE

Subsidiary angel: CALIEL

Farmers and agricultural workers

Ruling archangel: SACHIEL

Subsidiary angel: SOFIEL

Fashion, interior design, and skin care professionals

Ruling archangel: JOPHIEL

Subsidiary angel: ASMODEL

Fertility experts, IVF specialists, midwives, paediatricians, family therapists, obstetricians and gynaecologists, adoption and foster-care workers

Ruling archangel: SANDALPHON

Subsidiary angel: LAILAH OR MEBAHIAH

Film and television presenters, and masters of ceremonies
Ruling archangel: ZADKIEL
Subsidiary angel: CHUR

Firefighters and rescue workers
Ruling archangel: URIEL
Subsidiary angel: OCHIEL

Fishermen and women, dockers, and ferry workers
Ruling archangel: ARIEL
Subsidiary angel: RAHAB OR MANAKIEL

Fitness trainers and instructors, and all who work in health clubs and gyms
Ruling archangel: SAMAEL
Subsidiary angel: TRSIEL

Gardeners and horticulturists
Ruling archangel: ANAEL
Subsidiary angel: CATHAREL

Goldsmiths and all who work in the jewellery trade
Ruling archangel: URIEL
Subsidiary angel: OTHIAS

Grocers, greengrocers, organic producers, and supermarket workers
Ruling archangel: MICHAEL
Subsidiary angel: SAHALIAH

Hairdressers
Ruling archangel: CAMAEL
Subsidiary angel: ASMODEL

Hotel and hospitality workers, including bar staff
Ruling archangel: GABRIEL
Subsidiary angel: ARDOUSTA

Industrialists, factory and manufacturing workers
Ruling archangel: URIEL
Subsidiary angel: REMIEL

Journalists, newspaper editors and subeditors, reporters, television researchers and producers
Ruling archangel: SANDALPHON
Subsidiary angel: HARAHEL

Lawyers, solicitors, court officials, and judges
Ruling archangel: SACHIEL
Subsidiary angel: VASAIRIAH

Market researchers, workers with any data
Ruling archangel: GABRIEL
Subsidiary angel: NAHALIEL

Massage therapists, aromatherapists, and those giving hands-on treatments such as Reiki or reflexology
Ruling archangel: ZADKIEL
Subsidiary angel: EXAEL

Metalworkers and welders
Ruling archangel: MICHAEL
Subsidiary angel: KUTIEL

Military personnel
Ruling archangel: SAMAEL
Subsidiary angel: SAFRIEL

Musicians, singers, all connected with the music industry
Ruling archangel: SANDALPHON
Subsidiary angel: GABAMIAH

Negotiators, arbitrators, union officials, and peacemakers
Ruling archangel: SACHIEL
Subsidiary angel: GAVREEL

Night and shift workers
Ruling archangels: CASSIEL AND GABRIEL
Subsidiary angel: NATIEL

Nuclear and radiation workers, miners, earth and marine scientists
Ruling archangel: RAZIEL
Subsidiary angel: IMAMIAH

Office workers, secretaries
Ruling archangel: GABRIEL
Subsidiary angel: DANIEL

Opticians, ear specialists, dentists, and dental assistants
Ruling archangel: ZADKIEL
Subsidiary angel: NATIEL

Paramedics and ambulance drivers
Ruling archangel: AZRAEL
Subsidiary angel: ABDIEL

Pharmacists and herbalists
Ruling archangel: ANAEL
Subsidiary angel: SACHULPH

Photographers and the printing industry
Ruling archangel: JOPHIEL
Subsidiary angel: GALGALIEL

Pilots, airline staff, and cruise-ship workers
Ruling archangel: ARIEL
Subsidiary angel: DAMABIAH

Plumbers, drainage engineers, civil engineers
Ruling archangel: ARIEL
Subsidiary angel: NAHALIEL

Police, prison officers, and security guards
Ruling archangel: MICHAEL
Subsidiary angel: QAPHSIEL

Preschool and childcare workers
Ruling archangel: ANAEL
Subsidiary angel: AFRIEL

Priests and all those working in spiritually focused therapy businesses
Ruling archangel: METATRON
Subsidiary angel: HAHAZIAH

Psychologists, mental health workers, and psychiatrists
Ruling archangel: METATRON
Subsidiary angel: ATTARIB

Publishers, editors, proofreaders, authors, poets, and desktop publishers
Ruling archangel: METATRON
Subsidiary angel: MEHIEL

Railway workers and public transport employees
Ruling archangel: MICHAEL
Subsidiary angel: AMBRIEL

Real-estate agents, property developers, surveyors, and mortgage brokers
Ruling archangels: SACHIEL AND CASSIEL
Subsidiary angel: POEL

Sailors
Ruling archangel: MICHAEL
Subsidiary angel: DAMABIAH

Scientists
Ruling archangel: RAPHAEL
Subsidiary angel: URIM

Self-employment
Ruling archangel: RAPHAEL
Subsidiary angel: MAION

Shopkeepers and market traders
  Ruling archangel: RAPHAEL
  Subsidiary angel: SHAMSHIEL

Speculators, investors, stockbrokers, and risk assessors
  Ruling archangel: CASSIEL
  Subsidiary angel: IEILAEL

Spiritual healers and alternative health practitioners including homeopaths, Ayurveda, and traditional Chinese medicine practitioners
  Ruling archangel: ANAEL
  Subsidiary angel: ASSIEL

Surgeons
  Ruling archangel: CAMAEL
  Subsidiary angel: PADAEL

Teachers, lecturers, and students
  Ruling archangel: URIEL
  Subsidiary angel: HARAHEL

Translators, interpreters, and language teachers
  Ruling archangel: GABRIEL
  Subsidiary angel: OMAEL

Travel agents, tour guides or representatives, and everyone involved in the travel industry
  Ruling archangel: RAPHAEL
  Subsidiary angel: AMBRIEL

Veterinarians, animal rescue workers, animal trainers, communicators, and healers
  Ruling archangel: ARIEL
  Subsidiary angel: HARIEL

Women's aid workers, and all connected with women's matters and women's refuges

Ruling archangel: GABRIEL

Subsidiary angel: SHEKINAH

The "Fix-It" Angels

Of course, work is not only the nine-to-five routine in the office but all those other tasks, chores, and obstacles. Like the time your computer threatens to crash the one time you forget to back up your day's files, or you need to organise a taxi if you have worked late to avoid missing the last train. Or, when you do get home, you discover ten minutes before the shopping mall closes that your child has split her school shoes or needs fairy wings for a concert the next day ... and when you get to the mall, there's barely a parking space to be found.

In times of crisis, you can call on the transport angels, the parking angels, and the rest. Because the need is usually urgent, these obliging angels tend to be quite fast-acting. The following are angels I have found useful as a mother of five who has had to fit work around family life. But they can help whether you are working full time from home caring for a family or trying to juggle priorities and deadlines—and you still have to buy cat food!

Angels to call in difficult situations

AKATRIEL: Angel of talking your way out of a sticky situation

ASARIEL: Angel of fixing broken appliances in an emergency

BARIEL: Angel of car and vehicle problems, such as running out of fuel or urgently needing a taxi or bus

CATHAREL: Angel for making your salary last till pay day and feeding a family on a tight budget

ELEMIAH OR ADNACHIEL: Angel of safe driving when you are tired and stuck in traffic but need to be somewhere fast

GALGALIEL: Angel of parking and parking spaces

HAMAIEL: Angel of accounting and overdue tax returns and accounts

HUMIEL: Angel of home improvement and house renovation

JOPHIEL: Angel of keeping everyone happy at parties, birthdays, weddings, anniversaries, and garden and/or office parties

LAUVIAH: Angel of fixing computers and other technological problems

LUMIEL: Angel for sorting a crisis or panic at work

MANNA: Angel of cookery when you have to prepare a meal in a hurry

MEBAHEL: Angel of finances, visiting banks and applying for necessary loans, and also helping with debt problems

NITHAIAH: Angel of competitive sports and for when you are stranded away from home. Also angel of examinations and tests, of taking courses, or understanding instruction manuals; and of keys for when you get locked out or lose yours

ORIFIEL: Angel for turning a disastrous holiday or day out into fun

PADAEL: Angel for bad hair days and when absolutely everything goes wrong

ROCHEL OR RAHAB: Angel of finding lost things, pets, and people

SACHIEL: Angels for interviews of all kinds, employment issues, and getting a job fast

SAFRIEL: Angel for dealing with official matters, legal cases, and neighbourhood or workplace disputes

SU'IEL: Angel of small emergencies, such as finding a toilet urgently when out and about with a small child or getting a taxi late at night if your mobile phone will not work or all the taxi firms are booked solid

ZADKIEL: Angel of meeting deadlines and doing ten things at once

ZURIEL: Angel who prevents you from spending too much while shopping

THE COMPUTER ANGEL

Miranda, who lives in Southampton, was working on an important project on her laptop. She was almost finished when a virus warning flashed up. The antidote for that virus was only just available on the Internet. Miranda went quickly online to get the patch to fix it but she knew that if the screen went blank it would be too late and the hard drive contents would be wiped out. Unusually, Miranda had not backed up her work. The worst happened and the screen went blank.

Miranda did not know the name of the angel who would help but said, "Wherever you are, angels, please, please help. My job depends on this." At that moment, the screen sparked back into life though she hadn't touched it. She was able to apply the remedy and her work was saved.

THE LITERARY ANGEL

I was working in Sweden on a book and urgently needed a reference from an out-of-print American book. I had spent at least two hours in vain searching the Internet, but had drawn a blank. I asked Rahab, the angel of lost things and missing information, to help as I needed to track down the book by the end of the day.

I was at the point of giving up when Kajsa, the office manager, walked in holding a book that she thought might interest me, which she had found on her shelf at home. To my amazement, it was from the same American publisher I had been searching for.

Angel Meditations for Busy People

You can meditate absolutely anywhere, any time. This brief moment out of time will restore calm or give you a burst of energy and enthusiasm. However, if you barely have time to draw breath on the average day at work, let's start when you are not at work and maybe have time to get out into the open air. Then you can adapt the techniques you have learned to alleviate workplace stress.

Angelic meditation on the move

In this busy world, many people simply do not have time to sit and meditate. Fortunately, angelic meditations can be done on the move while walking, jogging, exercising, or in any daily task, with the exception of driving or cycling. It is possible to combine meditation with chores, though ideally nature is the best setting to fill you with its life force and those of different weather energies. The idea behind moving meditation is that a repetitive physical movement occupies your body and quiets the mind. Moving meditation is good for insomniacs or to help you switch off after a stressful day.

THE ON-THE-MOVE ANGEL MEDITATION

Choose a task when you are not too tired that will last for at least ten minutes, preferably longer. Swimming, walking, housework such as vacuuming, dancing to slow music, or cycling in the gym will create a naturally relaxed, semimeditative state.

+ Once you have established the rhythm, picture in your mind a shimmering gold and silver angel moving with you, just in front of you, facing you.

+ See the angelic form getting larger but remaining very fluid so it flows around you, making your own movements fluid. If doing housework, sprinkle dried lavender heads on the floor or rub furniture with an old-fashioned lavender and beeswax polish to bring in nature, and imagine petals from the flower angel falling all round you.

+ Create a soft mantra you can say aloud if you are alone, such as *"Move with me, wise angel, that I may travel through the realms of beauty and of nature and return restored."*

+ You may see or sense beautiful pastel mists and nature angels flying or floating slowly round you, and you will be filled with calm and purpose.

Three-minute meditations at work

Once you have mastered moving meditation, you can meditate for two or three minutes while sitting or standing, whether in a workspace, crowded bus, or train. If the scene is ugly, imagine a place of great natural beauty.

Meditating on rainbows

Rainbows dancing in the air or around a room when there is no natural light source are ways in which angels often make their presence felt. We met Iris, angel of rainbows, in chapter 5, though other angels are perceived with iridescent rainbow wings, such as Ariel, an archangel of nature who has rainbow robes, and Hahael, the angel of aid and charity workers, who has a rainbow halo. If you see a rainbow in the sky, take a minute or two to focus on its centre and you will feel a sense of joy and release, even if you are sad.

Create your own angel rainbow connection by hanging a lead or clear quartz crystal at one or more windows that catch the sun. If this is not possible, set a small clear quartz crystal sphere as a paperweight in your workspace. Buy one with lots of small cracks and hold it up to the light—it will reflect rainbows even in artificial light. You could download a beautiful rainbow photograph and save it as a screen saver. Alternatively, to tune into angelic rainbows visit a church with stained glass windows so that you can imagine the rainbow light from the windows filtering on the floor and colouring white statues whenever you need rainbow energy and you are in a dark, dull room.

The following rainbow meditation is one you can easily adapt to your workplace if you are feeling weighed down by negativity or by pettiness.

✖ THE RAINBOW ANGEL MEDITATION

+ If you are able to create rainbow colours in the office, relax and half-close your eyes and allow shimmering rainbow wings and the outline of a rainbow angel to form from the created rainbow light. If this seems hard, imagine an angelic outline behind the physical rainbow light that comes and goes out of vision as the rainbow colours move.

+ If using a crystal sphere, turn it very gently and focus on the inner rainbow.

+ Should you be in a workplace where you cannot make a physical rainbow, just blink and imagine rainbows in front of your eyes. Swirl a silver pen to catch the light. The only limit is your imagination.

+ Allow the rainbow angel to enfold you so you are seeing the workplace just for a minute or two through a rainbow haze, and say in your mind over and over, *"I am filled with the joy of the rainbow angel and nothing can depress or discourage me."*

+ After practising this for a few weeks, as soon as you recite your mantra in your mind, you may see rainbows invisible to everyone else.

An angelic power nap

This is a good substitute for the advised daily twenty-minute power nap when you have only a few minutes of peace.

1. To set up the experience, search the Internet for an ethereal, semiabstract angel image to download onto your computer, or buy a small poster of a classical painting of a beautiful angel. You can use different angel images, but they should always have flowing, indistinct lines.

2. To induce an angel power nap, stare hard at the picture for a minute or two and memorise every detail.

3. Then press your hands against your eyes and picture the image still as though you were looking at it.

4. Recreate the angel as if on a dark blue screen in your mind in every detail, step by step, as though you were painting the angel against the blue background.

5. Say as a mantra, *"Angel flow with me that I may go where there is peace and be restored."* Imagine you and the angel are moving hand in hand through the skies.

6. You may experience a sensation of gently floating through gentle blue skies, walking over cotton-wool clouds, or moving effortlessly in a velvety, star-studded navy universe.

7. Keep up this gentle swaying movement in your mind, reciting the words in your mind softer and slower until there is silence and stillness, and you are resting motionless, enclosed in soft, white wings.

8. You may feel as though you have been asleep for hours but usually no more than two or three minutes will have passed before some sound brings you back to full consciousness. Alternatively, when you feel restored, count slowly from twenty down to one, and on the count of three open your eyes and let the world return.

If you are an insomniac or if you are on a long-distance plane, coach, or train and need to sleep, you can download the image on to your mobile phone while out and about.

Angels will come into your working world if you invite them, and help in crises. They may take human form and in return, if you can help someone struggling, you increase the good vibes in the world. You may then become someone's rescuing working-day angel in a moment of need as well!

Elemental Nature Angels in the Workplace

Ideally, we would all go out into the fresh air during breaks at work, and some workplaces have an inner courtyard that serves as an office garden. Even city workers may have a small green square or park. But if you do not have the time to get outside, the angels of nature will come indoors to you.

Angels of nature wear the colours of the natural world that may subtly change in shade in the different seasons. Often they have wings, haloes, and robes of different shades of green, orange, or golden brown if they are connected with the earth; purple and white for sky angels, gold and red for fire angels, and blue or silver for water angels. These angels of earth, air, fire, and water act as a harmonising background energy.

For the earth angels who help to keep everything calm and focus on necessary details and schedules, have a leafy potted plant on your desk or a window ledge, a ceramic mug, or any brown or orange crystals in your workplace.

For the air angels and their communicative and entrepreneurial qualities, choose a small electric fan or a paper knife.

For the fire angels with their creative ideas and bursts of enthusiasm, have a small crystal sphere, a mirror, or any small reflective surface (stainless steel desk organizers are ideal, or a lead crystal on a chain at a nearby window to catch the light).

For the water angels, with their people skills and ability to cool down hot tempers, if you can, place fish in a tank in the office—this not only soothes, but according to feng shui, attracts prosperity to the workplace. Your mug filled with coffee or a bottle of mineral water is another good way of connecting with the water angels. Combine air and water with a deep bowl of water on which you drop fragrance oils (keep a bowl on a radiator to warm the water and diffuse the fragrance).

If you or other people are feeling lethargic (excess earth energy), ask for extra input from the fire angels. If there is a lot of sarcasm or backbiting (excess air energy), ask the earth angels to intervene. If tempers are fiery, then ask the water angels to bring reconciliation, and if people are being drama queens or kings or getting over-emotional, a quick dose of air-angel logic will restore the balance. You can touch an elemental focus, like water, a mirror, or your coffee mug, as detailed above, to release the relevant angelic elemental power whenever you need it.

seven

ZODIAC ANGELS

How often have you tried to arrange a family occasion, but have felt like the universe is conspiring against you? Or perhaps at work, you schedule a meeting on the day when everyone seems to be in a bad mood? As above in the skies, so below on earth, said ancient peoples—so if earthly plans seem to be hitting brick walls, why not consult the zodiac angels?

Each zodiac period has its own ruling angel. These zodiac angels can help you with planning your work, social or family life to ensure your meetings and dealings are productive and stress-free. Not only do zodiac angels assist those born under their sun sign, but they also rule one of the months of the year. The advantage of this is that they transfer the qualities of their zodiac period to a whole month that can be accessed by anyone during that month. Even more exciting for instant forward planning is that the moon passes through each of the star signs in turn for two and a half days each month. This means you can plan business or personal events during those two and a half-day periods using the different zodiac strengths of the angels, regardless of when you were born or the current calendar month. Following is an example so you can see how this could work for you.

SUZY'S ARIAN ANGEL

Suzy was born on 25 March and was a typical Aries—forthright, honest, always eager for action, and impatient with those who could not keep up. Her zodiac angel was Machidiel, and once she connected with him, he kept her energies balanced. This helped Suzy to display her creative energies in the advertising agency where she worked, but played down her less tactful Arian excesses that had made her previously essential but not well liked.

However, Suzy became aware that Greg, a new executive based in America (also an Arian), disliked her intensely. People of the same sign can clash initially, but sometimes they do settle down into an understanding because they share the same enthusiasms. This didn't happen in Suzy's case; though they mainly communicated by phone, their conversations were often sharp and terse, and Suzy dreaded Greg's trips to London for meetings.

One day over a business lunch, the conversation was different—sparky and creative but with none of the usual confrontation in their dialogues. Suzy could not understand the change in Greg's attitude until she checked her diary, which showed moon phases, and realised that the day and time of the meeting was when the moon had moved into Aries.

Now, when possible, Suzy fixes any vital contact between them during the two and a half days a month when the moon is in Aries, or chooses the phase of a softer sign such as the moon in Libra, which tends to encourage harmony and detachment of emotions. Of course, Suzy never tells the sceptical Greg about her celestial management, but even encounters at less auspicious times have become less confrontational.

Working with the Zodiac Angels

I have briefly described the zodiac angels according to traditional imagery, but as you work with and make more personal connections with them, you may perceive them differently. Trust yourself. Your own zodiacal angel is the most important to confirm, and it can strengthen your identity at any time of the year, so wear your personal zodiac crystal or colour listed (see pages 129–136) whenever you need to accentuate your core qualities. However, you can borrow zodiac crystals and fragrances if you are using particular moon zodiac periods regularly (the two and a half days in the month when the moon is in the appropriate zodiac sign).

Light your personal zodiac candle and burn your astrofragrance as incense or oils, or have the natural flowers of your sign at home or work whenever you need a boost. Alternatively, use your personal crystal elixir in drinks, in baths, or splashed on your energy-centre points as I describe at this end of this chapter (see page 148).

You can easily put zodiacal angel information in your diary or mobile phone planner, so you will know the current moon zodiac period and which angel's energies can help at a particular time. This information is good for advance planning to help ensure a less stressful social, work, or family life. You can find it online, in the astrology or weather sections of newspapers, or in an almanac that gives the moon phases.

Your Birth Guardian Angels and Their Zodiac Correspondences

Aries 🐏

SYMBOL: The ram

DATES: 21 March–20 April

RULING ANGEL: Machidiel (or Malahidael), warrior angel with sparkling golden-red halo and wings

STRENGTHS: Self-confidence, strong identity, innovation, assertiveness, action

CHALLENGES: Impatience, irritability, being abrupt

QUALITIES BROUGHT TO THOSE NOT BORN UNDER THIS SIGN: Acting confidently

COLOUR: Red

CRYSTALS: Carnelian, diamond, Herkimer diamond

INCENSES OR OILS: Cedar, cinnamon, dragon's blood

FLOWERS: Geranium, hibiscus, hollyhock, honeysuckle, tiger lily

COMPATIBILITY CLASH: Libra

Taurus

SYMBOL: The bull

DATES: 21 April–21 May

RULING ANGEL: Asmodel or Ashmodel, angel of beauty, surrounded by pink rays, creating what is of worth

STRENGTHS: Persistence, patience, reliability, loyalty, practical abilities, stability, love of beauty

CHALLENGES: Stubbornness, occasional flashes of temper, over-concern with material things

QUALITIES BROUGHT TO THOSE NOT BORN UNDER THIS SIGN: Inner radiance, valuing your own beauty, and ignoring anyone who makes you feel bad

COLOUR: Pink

CRYSTALS: Emerald, rose quartz

INCENSES AND OILS: Apple blossom, rose

FLOWERS: Columbine, daisy, foxglove, poppy, primula, rose, violet

COMPATIBILITY CLASH: Scorpio

Gemini

SYMBOL: The heavenly twins

DATES: 22 May–21 June

RULING ANGEL: Ambriel or Ambiel, the messenger and travel angel, wearing colours of early morning sunlight

STRENGTHS: Excellent communication skills, adaptability, scientific/ technological aptitude, curiosity, intelligence, versatility

CHALLENGES: Restlessness, sarcasm, over-logical thinking

QUALITIES BROUGHT TO THOSE NOT BORN UNDER THIS SIGN: Lateral thinking and alternative perspectives, ability to look further afield for what you need

COLOURS: Pale yellow and grey

CRYSTALS: Citrine, white sapphire

INCENSES AND OILS: Lavender, lemon grass

FLOWERS: Azalea, chrysanthemum, lavender, lilac, lily of the valley, orchid

COMPATIBILITY CLASH: Sagittarius

Cancer

SYMBOL: The crab

DATES: 22 June–22 July

RULING ANGEL: Muriel, the silvery and pearl-robed healer angel with her magic carpet of dreams

STRENGTHS: Sensitivity, kindness, imagination, natural flair for home-making, nurturing (especially of children), creating emotional security, ability to keep secrets

CHALLENGES: Over-defensiveness, secrecy, worrying unnecessarily about home and loved ones

QUALITIES BROUGHT TO THOSE NOT BORN UNDER THIS SIGN: Sensitivity to the unexpressed needs and feelings of others

COLOUR: Silver

CRYSTALS: Moonstone or pearl

INCENSES AND OILS: Jasmine, lemon balm

FLOWERS: Lily, lotus, magnolia, sea lavender, small white flowers stocks

COMPATIBILITY CLASH: Capricorn

Leo

SYMBOL: The lion

DATES: 23 July–23 August

RULING ANGEL: Verchiel (or Verachiel), the golden joy-bringer who is surrounded by sunbeams

STRENGTHS: Power, courage, generosity, nobility, idealism, leadership, protection of the weak, ability to perform creatively in public

CHALLENGES: Drama king or queen, autocracy, occasionally cruelty

QUALITIES BROUGHT TO THOSE NOT BORN UNDER THIS SIGN: Ambition and impetus to strive for happiness and success

COLOUR: Gold

CRYSTALS: Clear crystal quartz, golden topaz

INCENSES AND OILS: Copal (a plant or tree resin), frankincense, orange

FLOWERS: Aster, dahlia, marigold, passion flower, potted palms, sunflower

COMPATIBILITY CLASH: Aquarius

Virgo

SYMBOL: The maiden

DATES: 24 August–22 September

RULING ANGEL: Hamaliel or Hamaiel, angel of perfection, surrounded by misty forest green

STRENGTHS: Striving for perfection, organisational skills, methodical, attention to detail, efficiency, healing powers, ability to persevere a routine, but necessary, task through to the end; reliability

CHALLENGES: Fussiness, hypochondria, becoming over-obsessed by details and missing the bigger picture

QUALITIES BROUGHT TO THOSE NOT BORN UNDER THIS SIGN: Ability to work hard, to complete necessary and boring paperwork, and not panic in a crisis

COLOUR: Green

CRYSTALS: Jade, moss agate, opal, peridot

INCENSES AND OILS: moss, musk, patchouli

FLOWERS: Iris, moss, narcissus, pansy, periwinkle, small yellow flowers, sweet pea

COMPATIBILITY CLASH: Pisces

Libra

SYMBOL: The scales

DATES: 23 September–23 October

RULING ANGEL: Zuriel, the teacher, the pale-blue angel who brings calm and reason to any situation

STRENGTHS: Harmony, ability to see both sides of a situation, diplomacy, peacemaking skills, a strong sense of justice and charisma

CHALLENGES: Tendency to sit on the fence, indecisiveness in an emergency, flirtatiousness

QUALITIES BROUGHT TO THOSE NOT BORN UNDER THIS SIGN: Preventing unwise and impulsive words or actions that may be regretted

COLOUR: Light blue

CRYSTALS: Blue sapphire, blue topaz, lapis lazuli

INCENSES AND OILS: Lemon verbena, peach, vanilla

FLOWERS: blue flowers, ferns, hydrangea, lupin, Michaelmas daisy, pot roses, rhododendron

COMPATIBILITY CLASH: Aries

Scorpio

SYMBOL: The scorpion

DATES: 24 October–22 November

RULING ANGEL: Bariel, the angel of small miracles, who wears the colours of sunset

STRENGTHS: Intensity; religious, spiritual, and psychic awareness; ability to transform self and situations; the power to start over again or revive a stagnant situation

CHALLENGES: Obsessive, inability to let go of the past, especially past wrongs; spite for spite's sake

QUALITIES BROUGHT TO THOSE NOT BORN UNDER THIS SIGN: Help in times of need and a reminder not to repeat past mistakes or scenarios

COLOURS: Burgundy, indigo

CRYSTALS: aqua aura, black pearl, coral, obsidian

INCENSES AND OILS: Mimosa, mint, pine

FLOWERS: Anemone, cactus, gardenia, heather, snapdragon, spiky flowering plants

COMPATIBILITY CLASH: Taurus

Sagittarius

SYMBOL: The archer

DATES: 23 November–21 December

RULING ANGEL: Adnachiel or Advachiel, the angel of learning and exploration, with bright yellow robes

STRENGTHS: Expansiveness, love of travel and exploration, clear vision, seeking truth, wide perspectives, flexibility, open-mindedness, optimism, enthusiasm, creativity, especially in writing

CHALLENGES: Tactlessness, inability to focus on one project or person, tendency to "throw out the baby with the bathwater"

QUALITIES BROUGHT TO THOSE NOT BORN UNDER THIS SIGN: Learning new things and visiting new places; a good travelling companion

COLOUR: Bright yellow

CRYSTALS: Ruby, turquoise

INCENSES AND OILS: Sage, sandalwood

FLOWERS: All tropical exotic flowers, dandelion, dried grasses, oleander, peony

COMPATIBILITY CLASH: Gemini

Capricorn

SYMBOL: The half-goat, half-fish

DATES: 22 December–20 January

RULING ANGEL: Anael or Hanael, the protector and archangel of love and fidelity, surrounded by green, silver, and roses

STRENGTHS: Wise caution, persistence regardless of opposition, respecter of tradition, ambition, self-discipline, loyalty, fidelity and prudence with financial affairs

CHALLENGES: Over-cautiousness, meanness, inability to adapt to new situations and people, inability to accept being in the wrong

QUALITIES BROUGHT TO THOSE NOT BORN UNDER THIS SIGN: Valuing love and fidelity over excitement, persevering when the going gets tough

COLOURS: Indigo, brown

CRYSTALS: Garnet, ruby, titanium aura

INCENSES AND OILS: Cypress, magnolia, myrrh

FLOWERS: , Christmas rose, holly, hyacinth, ivy, poinsettia

COMPATIBILITY CLASH: Cancer

Aquarius

SYMBOL: The water carrier

DATES: 21 January–18 February

RULING ANGEL: Cambiel, tall, shadowy watcher or guardian archangel, guards you day and night from your own mistakes as well as external dangers

STRENGTHS: Idealism, independence, humanitarianism, inventiveness, detachment from swings of emotion or prejudices, unique perspective on the world

CHALLENGES: Inability to feel or show empathy for others, eccentricity and crankiness

QUALITIES BROUGHT TO THOSE NOT BORN UNDER THIS SIGN: The ability to detach from unnecessary emotion or emotional pressures, assessing the right moment to act

COLOURS: Dark blue, purple

CRYSTALS: Amethyst, blue lace agate, zircon

INCENSES AND OILS: Benzoin, lemon, rosemary

FLOWERS: Crocus, snowdrop, sprouting flower bulbs or hothouse flowers such as the orchid, violet

COMPATIBILITY CLASH: Leo

Pisces

SYMBOL: The fish

DATES: 19 February–20 March

RULING ANGEL: Barakiel or Barchiel, the blue and gold archangel of lightning and good luck, who has lightning flashing from his halo

STRENGTHS: Evolved intuitive powers, sympathy and empathy with others, weaver of myths, awareness of hidden factors, ability to merge with surroundings, alternative spirituality

CHALLENGES: Sentimentality, excess emotions, change ability according to who is present

QUALITIES BROUGHT TO THOSE NOT BORN UNDER THIS SIGN: Spontaneity, imagination and ability to read people

COLOURS: mauve, soft white

CRYSTALS: Bloodstone, coral, fluorite

INCENSES AND OILS: Honeysuckle, lotus, sweet grass

FLOWERS: Daffodil, early spring flowers, water lily, wisteria

COMPATIBILITY CLASH: Virgo

Month Angels

Each month also has its ruling angel. Month angels endow their months with their own strengths. This means particular months are especially good for certain ventures or occasions such as weddings, adventure, holidays, or even a conference. The month angels also indicate by the inherent weaknesses of each zodiac sign what should best be avoided during specific months (or at least compensated for). This knowledge can aid with forward planning. If, for example, you wanted to start your own business, January would be ideal as this is the month most favoured for self-employment. This is because it is ruled by Cambiel, the watcher, and the angel of independent ventures, who is in his other role the zodiac angel of Aquarius (21 January–18 February). However, you also have the benefit that though January is Cambiel's month from beginning to end, the previous zodiac angel Anael, the angel of cautious Capricorn energies (22 December–20 January) also has energies present to a lesser extent from 1–20 January. This means you could do all the final planning or finances in early January when Anael steadies and consolidates in the background, and plan the launch of the company for 21 January or wait until 31 January, when you get the double dose of Cambiel independence and original creative energies.

A month is always ruled by its own angel, but be sure to check which zodiac angel also has influence, as there may be beneficial overlapping zodiac energies. For a wedding, go for the first half of July, the month of Verchiel, the joy bringer, who also rules Leo (23 July–23 August). He will make sure that it is a day to remember, as Verchiel is a showman through and through. However, since this is a wedding and not a Hollywood production, you will benefit if you wed between 1–22 July with the softer, romantic Cancerian energies of Muriel (22 June–22 July) in the background. She is also good for calming difficult relatives or factions that might emerge to sour the day. Of course, if you wanted a quiet romantic wedding, the second half of Muriel's June would be better as you would get a double dose of romance.

I have already listed the different angels' crystals and other associations under the zodiac associations (see pages 129–136). Check back, as you will use these for the month each angel rules. You could burn Verchiel gold candles and have gold-edged table settings at the wedding reception, carry a bouquet of golden and yellow flowers, and maybe wear tiny clear crystal beads sewn on your headdress at your July wedding.

January

CAMBIEL THE WATCHER, ANGEL OF JANUARY AND AQUARIUS
  (21 JANUARY–18 FEBRUARY)

GOOD FOR: Independent ventures; launching projects and self-employment; joining groups; entering competitions, raffles and lotteries

AVOID: Seeking or offering commitment in love; family celebrations; initiating joint projects; dealing with emotional or sensitive family affairs

February

BARAKIEL (OR BARCHIEL) THE BRINGER OF GOOD LUCK, ANGEL OF FEBRUARY AND PISCES (19 FEBRUARY–20 MARCH)

GOOD FOR: Resolving conflicts; reconciliations; combining two careers or interests; psychic development; changing bad luck; emotional matters; overseas travel

AVOID: Encounters with officialdom; committing yourself to binding contracts; matters involving logic or attention to detail; people who are manipulative

March

MACHIDIEL (OR MALAHIDAEL) THE INNOVATOR, ANGEL OF MARCH AND ARIES (21 MARCH–20 APRIL)

GOOD FOR: Action-packed holidays and getting fit; tackling bullies or inequality; passionate love; initiating or launching new projects

AVOID: Negotiations with intolerant people; activities involving perseverance; working as a lesser team member; being restricted physically or following a rigid training programme

April

ASMODEL, THE CREATOR OF WHAT IS OF WORTH, ANGEL OF APRIL AND TAURUS (21 APRIL–21 MAY)

GOOD FOR: Makeovers and healthy eating regimes; graceful exercise; creative arts; visiting beautiful places, spending time in nature, making your workspace harmonious

AVOID: Noisy, soulless environments; arguing on matters of principle; trying to economise unless absolutely necessary

May

AMBRIEL OR AMBIEL, THE MESSENGER AND TRAVELLER, ANGEL OF MAY AND GEMINI (22 MAY–21 JUNE)

GOOD FOR: Changing jobs; learning new skills; short-term / distance travel and house moves; public speaking; interviews; tests; media work; speculation

AVOID: Boring situations; making long-term plans or commitments; organising get-togethers; staying with relatives; trying to please others; exaggerating—you may be found out this month

June

MURIEL THE HEALER, ANGEL OF JUNE AND CANCER (22 JUNE–22 JULY)

GOOD FOR: Sensitive family issues; contacting an estranged friend or relative; imaginative projects; homemaking or DIY projects; starting a counselling or spiritual career; welcoming new family members; conceiving a baby, fertility tests, or treatment

AVOID: Entertaining those you do not know well; sharing secrets; staying in unfamiliar places; disruptions to routine; holding on to people or situations when it is time to let go

July

VERCHIEL THE JOY BRINGER, ANGEL OF JULY AND LEO
   (23 JULY–23 AUGUST)

GOOD FOR: Taking the lead; launching a major ambition; entering talent shows or reality television series; applying for promotion or a pay rise; marriage proposals; exotic holidays in the sun

AVOID: Overspending; overindulging in food or alcohol; starting a love affair you may regret by next month

August

HAMALIEL THE PERFECTIONIST, ANGEL OF AUGUST AND VIRGO
   (24 AUGUST–22 SEPTEMBER)

GOOD FOR: Major cleaning, reorganising, or using feng shui in the home or workplace; trying new health supplements and alternative treatments; doing paperwork; starting a new budget

AVOID: Getting overtired and stressed; setting yourself impossible targets; being too fussy and refusing to accept anything or anyone less than perfect; trying to force children or partners along a road that may not be right for them

September

ZURIEL THE TEACHER, ANGEL OF SEPTEMBER AND LIBRA
   (23 SEPTEMBER–23 OCTOBER)

GOOD FOR: Justice, whether legal or personal; resolving gender, ageist, or sexist inequalities in the workplace; quiet holidays or relaxing weekends; marriage and long-term commitments

AVOID: Taking sides or being railroaded into giving an opinion; flirting or falling for flattery and con-merchants; trying to live a double life—especially in love

October

BARIEL OR BARUEL, THE WISE ONE AND ANGEL OF SMALL MIRACLES, ANGEL OF OCTOBER AND SCORPIO (24 OCTOBER–22 NOVEMBER)

GOOD FOR: Discovering the truth; visiting places you feel spiritually drawn to; ending relationships, legal separations, divorces or terminating contracts; starting again in a new place or career; developing clairvoyance; finding your soul mate or reviving an intense relationship; getting what you really want

AVOID: Repeating past mistakes; extreme exercise regimes or crash diets; joining any organisation or religion that may be obsessive or manipulative; sulking instead of sharing your feelings

November

ADNACHIEL THE VOYAGER, ANGEL OF NOVEMBER AND SAGITTARIUS (23 NOVEMBER–21 DECEMBER)

GOOD FOR: Long-distance travel, holidays, and house moves (especially relocation abroad); learning new skills; changing career direction; writing a novel or sending it for publication

AVOID: Giving unasked-for opinions; impulsive words or actions; being tempted by too-good-to-be-true offers; gambling or assuming the grass is greener on the other side

December

ANAEL OR HANAEL THE PROTECTOR AND ANGEL OF LOVE AND FIDELITY, ANGEL OF DECEMBER AND CAPRICORN (22 DECEMBER– 20 JANUARY)

GOOD FOR: All plans and detailed preparations; exploring your family tree; taking financial advice; being cautious with money; reviving old friendships; spending time with older relatives; also for any slow moving official matters

AVOID: Mean people; socialising for the sake of it; getting bogged down in routine; taking on responsibilities that are not yours or that you will later resent

Zodiac Angels and the Moon

Every month, the moon passes through the zodiac signs and spends about two and a half days in each. You can instantly draw on particular angelic zodiacal energies during any month—such as a burst of Machidiel Arian courage, for example, when the moon is in Aries. These brief monthly zodiac periods are also good for helping people of the same sign to get on better, or for you to harmonise with those whose sign is in opposition to yours. If you are meeting anyone who causes you problems, try to find out their zodiac sign and arrange a time when the moon is midway between your two signs. As with all instances, ask the ruling angels to mediate, adding their colours, flowers, or crystal elixirs (see below) in equal measure to harmonise the energies.

During the two and a half days each month that the moon passes through a sign, the emphasis of the energies will vary according to whether the moon is waxing, waning, or full. Let's therefore add three of the main moon angels who will work alongside the zodiac angels.

The waxing moon: Gabriel, archangel of the moon, rules the fifth day after the new moon (refer to your diary or check online to find the new moon, as the date varies each month). Pictured with a crescent-moon silver halo and dressed in starry blue or silver, he will help your zodiac angel from days 1 to 13 of the moon cycle, increasing any positive energy.

Gabriel's candle colour is silver. You could light this along with the candle of the appropriate zodiacal angel to blend their energies.

The full moon: Ofaniel has a hundred pairs of silver wings and rules from days 14 to 17, initiating change or bringing completion to the zodiac energies during his temporary rule as the moon whizzes through the month. His candle colour is white.

The waning moon: Amutiel rules from day 18 to the end of the moon month. She is pictured as a mature angel with pure white robes, pale shimmering blue halo, and wings. She helps us let go of anything holding us back and to withdraw from conflict or stress. Her candle colour is pearly grey.

Zodiacal and Lunar Angelic Powers

If possible, fix meetings, events, or dates so they fall within the best zodiac influence during the month. If the moon is waxing when you need it to be waning, ask the waning moon angel to help, and ask the waxing angel to replace what you are removing with something good.

+ Name the appropriate angels, ask their blessings and then state your need or purpose as you light their candles on the day or evening the moon enters the relevant sign. (Again, check online, in a diary that gives moon movements, or in an astrological almanac or ephemeris for the monthly moon movements through the signs.)

+ You can also write your wish or need in the air over both candles with the smoke of an incense stick (use either one of the incenses of the zodiac angel ruling at that time, or myrrh or jasmine for the moon).

+ Then either leave the candles and incense to burn through for a slow or more long-term matter, or if you want an instant infusion of power, blow out the candle, saying, *"So may it be."*

Moon in Aries

ZODIACAL ANGEL: Machidiel

WAXING: For courage, independence, self-reliance, self-employment, action, health, assertiveness, launching major ventures or life changes, energy, and passion

FULL: For an all-out survival effort or a major leap to overcome a huge obstacle

WANING: Antibullying and aggressiveness, and to reduce hyperactivity

Moon in Taurus

ZODIACAL ANGEL: Asmodel

WAXING: For fertility, love, radiance, money, material security, and to acquire beautiful things

FULL MOON: For conception of a child, getting a lover to commit, or for a major money venture

WANING: For losing weight, overcoming possessiveness and emotional blackmail, reducing debt, protecting possessions

Moon in Gemini

ZODIACAL ANGEL: Ambriel

WAXING: For speculation and games of chance, passing tests, healing using surgery or medical intervention, communication, travel and moves of all kinds; also for good luck

FULL MOON: For taking a necessary risk, unresponsive health problems, and successful dealings with the media

WANING: For protection against deceit, gossip, and spite; and to reverse bad luck

Moon in Cancer

ZODIACAL ANGEL: Muriel

WAXING: For happiness at home, family, children and fidelity; also for keeping secrets

FULL MOON: For conceiving a baby, overcoming relationship problems or betrayal, and for major home projects

WANING: For protection of the home and family against accidents or hostile neighbours

Moon in Leo

ZODIACAL ANGEL: Verchiel

WAXING: For success, power, leadership, fame, prosperity, career, abundance, potency, childbirth

FULL MOON: For a job interview or promotion, a chance to shine and overcome a challenge to your authority

WANING: For reducing negative effects of critical people, overcoming problems with bosses, and financial shortages and losses

Moon in Virgo

ZODIACAL ANGEL: Hamaliel

WAXING: For health and healing matters, animals, striving for perfection, employment, skill with hands, gardening, the environment, and for keeping to diets

FULL MOON: For striving to be the best in your field and for a major spring clean or overhaul of your everyday world

WANING: For banishing illness and any form of addiction or compulsion, helping clumsy children or adults, overcoming unemployment, and for personal safety

Moon in Libra

ZODIACAL ANGEL: Zuriel

WAXING: For marriage and partnerships, harmony, justice, successful outcome of court cases, sociability, charisma, and compromise

FULL MOON: For righting a major injustice, resolving or restoring balance to a partnership or marriage crisis, finding the perfect match in love or business

WANING: Use to prevent lack of commitment, infidelity, laziness and inertia, and in antiwar and conflict empowerments

Moon in Scorpio

ZODIACAL ANGEL: Bariel

WAXING: For transformation, wishes, passionate sex; to increase psychic powers and for any strongly felt desires or needs; for recovering what has been lost or stolen

FULL MOON: For sacred sex and the consummation of committed lovers and any urgent wish or desire

WANING: For protection against physical, emotional, or psychic attack, to guard against anyone seeking revenge, protection against vandalism, jealousy and being the victim of criminal activity

Moon in Sagittarius

ZODIACAL ANGEL: Adnachiel

WAXING: For travel, adventures, house moves, horses, publishing and creative ventures, happiness and optimism, good ideas, sports, and for finding lost pets.

FULL MOON: For major travel plans, long-distance holidays, or urgent house moves

WANING: Protection on journeys and against getting lost, preventing pets straying or being stolen, slowing or reversing money losses

Moon in Capricorn

ZODIACAL ANGEL: Anael or Hanael

WAXING: For long-term commitment in love; financial security; official matters; caution; steady career success; stable business ventures and slow-growing investments; perseverance and overcoming obstacles through persistent effort

FULL MOON: For overcoming a seemingly insurmountable object or opposition, operating within limitations, or starting again after failure or a major setback

WANING: For overcoming depression and self-doubt and releasing money that is tied up or disputed

Moon in Aquarius

ZODIACAL ANGEL: Cambiel

WAXING: For original ventures, success of inventions, intellectual matters, humanitarian issues, friendships, developing unique gifts and talents, and for alternative medicine

FULL MOON: For an original solution to a long-standing problem, major world aid or peace needs, launching a second career based on an innate but previously undeveloped talent

WANING: For overcoming intolerance, bad habits, prejudice, and inequality, and for banishing loneliness and isolation

Moon in Pisces

ZODIACAL ANGEL: Barakiel

WAXING: For new love; music and the performing arts; balancing two commitments or careers; fertility; adaptability; merging two families; and for telepathic powers

FULL MOON: For making an intuitive leap, proof of psychic abilities, doing two things or following two careers at once

WANING: For overcoming rivalries and people pulling you in different directions; reconciling quarrels, custody, or divorce disputes; and for overcoming excesses or imbalances of any kind

Making angelic zodiac crystal elixirs

Crystal elixirs are empowered waters that have been filled with the angelic and spiritual energy of the different zodiacal crystals. Add them to drinks to fill you with your own zodiacal power any time of the year or to tune into monthly energies if you feel tired or dispirited. If made and drunk when the moon is in a certain sign, you can get an instant infusion of that zodiacal energy.

Zodiacal elixirs also help if you need to borrow a zodiacal strength from another sign, and by using two or more crystals, you can mix together the zodiacal energies of different people to bring harmony in love or business.

A second method is suggested if you are anxious for any reason about drinking crystal-infused water, as in this method the crystal does not enter the water.

Please note that not all crystals are suitable for crystal elixirs—see the safety note on page 150 for a list of those to avoid.

Carry your angelic zodiac-infused water in a mineral water bottle or flask to work or to sports or social events. Make the elixir during the relevant star-sign period, the month the zodiac angel rules or when the moon is in a particular star sign. The full moon is an especially potent time for making zodiac elixirs.

Making crystal elixirs

One small rounded polished crystal, the size of an average coin, will infuse about 17 fluid ounces of water. Two will make 200–225 ounces and three up to a litre, increasing proportionately for larger quantities. Crystal waters keep their full power for about twenty-four hours after the crystal is removed, but for domestic or workplace use, you can keep them for two days afterwards.

✿ METHOD 1

1. Wash the chosen crystal(s) under running water, naming in your mind or aloud the zodiacal angel(s) who rules each crystal and the specific energies you need.

2. Place them in the water using a spoon or tongs. Still mineral or distilled/filtered water is good but you can substitute tap water for larger quantities, for animals, or for sprinkling around the home or your workspace.

3. Cover the container or put the cap back on the bottle.

4. Hold the sealed container between your hands, repeating the purpose of the elixir, and ask again that the zodiac angel or angels will bless the water: *"For the greatest good and with the purest intentions."*

5. Leave the covered water and crystals in the refrigerator overnight.

6. Pour the water into suitable containers in the morning, removing the crystal(s) with tongs or a spoon. Allow the crystals to dry and keep them in an open container to be filled with natural light until you need them again.

Alternatively, infuse the crystal water outdoors (or near a window) with sunlight or moonlight. You can make an elixir in three hours if the crystal water is left in bright sunlight or moonlight.

🜚 METHOD 2

1. In a large glass bowl containing water, float a small glass container (like an old, well-washed make-up pot with a screw-top lid, removing the lid first).

2. Wash the crystals and ask the help of the associated angels.

3. Hold each crystal in turn, adding one at a time to your cupped hands. Repeat the purpose of the crystal elixir and ask each of the ruling zodiac angel(s) to infuse the mix with the most positive aspects of the star sign and to minimise the more challenging aspects.

4. Now drop the crystals one by one into the container (not the water), saying for each crystal, *"May you be blessed and bring blessings by the angel ... (name them)."* Seal or cover the inner container.

5. Cover the bowl or put fine mesh across so it cannot become polluted.

6. Leave the bowl in sunlight for three days, outdoors if at all possible, or near a window that catches a lot of light.

7. Fill bottles with the water and use as appropriate.

Using zodiac crystal waters

+ Leave an infused glass of your personal water by your bed to drink as soon as you wake to get your day off to a good start.

+ Add your zodiacal crystal water to baths, wet a washcloth, or add to shampoo or shower gel. For example, Taurus rose quartz angel water will reduce stress.

♦ Splash it on your hairline, brow, throat, and inner wrists to refresh you during the day and give you a sense of well-being if you feel tired, pressured, or lethargic.

♦ To bring harmony and encourage connections between different family members—especially new ones if you have step-family members or are inviting new in-laws—make tea, coffee, or cold drinks with elixir water for anyone present, or add when making a cake or casserole using the relevant zodiac crystals. At a workplace meeting, put the water in small jugs or glasses round the table or even add to flower water. In this way, the particular properties of the elixir can enter the aura of those present or be absorbed by the flowers to fill the air with calm or enthusiasm, according to the crystal elixir you choose. For example, Gemini citrine elixir will fill everyone with good ideas and promote clear and positive communication.

Use the angel waters during their own months to give you the strengths of the month. If the month energies are wrong for your purpose, you can transfer the angelic energy of a more suitable month angel. For example, you could drink Barakiel Aquarian/February good-luck amethyst water if you need good luck or to reverse a run of bad luck (check the lists above for the appropriate crystals).

IMPORTANT SAFETY NOTE ON CRYSTAL ELIXIRS

Azurite, cinnabar, copper in any form, coral, malachite, meteorite, halite, crocoites, vandanite, and fuchsite are *not* considered suitable for crystal elixirs. If you are not sure if a crystal is porous or potentially toxic, always use method 2.

eight

AN ANGEL
FOR EVERY DAY

We all have an angel who rules our birthday, endowing us with particular qualities and gifts. Each birthday angel rules a block of five days. The three angels of your star sign, birth month, and birthday are the cosmic version of your personal angelic team. Sometimes, because of the way your birthday falls in the month, your birth month and star sign angels may be the same.

Your Birthday Gifts

Your birthday angel brings special gifts and talents, helping you understand why you have an affinity with certain careers or personality traits yet to be developed. Listed in the next section are the birthday angels' gifts as well as what each five-day period is good or not so favourable for in your everyday life, regardless of when you were born (day *strengths* and day *weaknesses*). Look for particular days that favour best energies for certain activities, events, or meetings and avoid certain activities on nonfavourable days.

If you want to carry a lucky crystal, light a candle, or wear a particular colour to strengthen your determination on a certain day, find the chosen day's ruling zodiac angel associations and symbols listed in chapter 7 (pages 129–136). So if, for example, you wanted to conclude a property deal on 7 January, which is a good day for this, you would use Anael or Hanael's candles or colours, as that day's angel, Ieilael, comes under the influence of Anael or Hanael, who rules from 22 December–20 January. Therefore, the best colours for 7 January would be indigo or brown, and the lucky crystals are garnet, ruby, and titanium aura.

January 1–5

NEMAMIAH stands at the gates of the new year. He guards the very old, children, animals, and any who are vulnerable.

GIFTS: The ability to recreate and transform what is imperfect to more perfect forms and so move forward creatively.

STRENGTHS: New energies sweeping in for changes and choices.

WEAKNESSES: Be careful not to act with undue haste.

January 6–10

IEILAEL encourages caution and preparation, laying the foundations of security and stability, and conserving finances for the future.

GIFTS: Having an old head on young shoulders from childhood and the power to forward-plan and make wise financial investments.

STRENGTHS: A property deal or house move can be initiated.

WEAKNESSES: Sort out your finances and if necessary seek advice.

January 11–15

HARAEL, called the shining one, is patron of schools, libraries, colleges, universities, archives, and museums. He also encourages the use of traditional knowledge to make discoveries about the past to guide the future.

GIFTS: The ability to take the best from the past but not be bound by it; having a natural gift for history and research.

STRENGTHS: Excellent for discovering family roots.

WEAKNESSES: Do not resist learning new skills.

January 16–20

MITZRAEL encourages the spread of freedom of speech, action and equality for women and oppressed minorities.

GIFTS: Respect for every individual; not seeking instant popularity, but having valuable lifelong friends.

STRENGTHS: Loyal friends and family will give immense support and pleasure.

WEAKNESSES: Beware of revealing too much to an exciting but unreliable new friend.

January 21–25

UMABEL rules over the physical sciences, astronomy, and space exploration and encourages wise discrimination both for individuals and on a global level.

GIFTS: The ability to see and move beyond what is instantly gratifying to what is of lasting worth.

STRENGTHS: Good for a major purchase where quality and durability is of the essence.

WEAKNESSES: Look round for a better deal or adviser.

January 26–30

IAHHEL is an angel of light who watches over all who work or live alone.

GIFTS: Individuality, the ability to create and fulfil personal destiny without measuring success against others' achievements.

STRENGTHS: Excellent for self-employment or solo ventures.

WEAKNESSES: Do not let others put you down.

January 31–February 4

ANAUEL guides those who work in commercial, property, and financial organisations to act with integrity, and campaigns that everyone will have a good standard of living.

GIFTS: Being one of life's social campaigners and the ability to combine a social conscience with personal success and abundance.

STRENGTHS: Good for claiming allowances and getting home improvement or work enterprise grants.

WEAKNESSES: Avoid lending anything that will not be returned.

February 5–9

MEHIEL rules writers, poets, public speakers, researchers, and lecturers, especially new or struggling ones. He supports wise censorship of what might corrupt the young.

GIFTS: High standards personally and the potential to become an effective, successful professional communicator and disseminator of knowledge.

STRENGTHS: A good day to take centre stage, to speak out, and for any influential meetings.

WEAKNESSES: A lot of people are talking a lot of rubbish. Speak out; you know better.

February 10–14

DAMABIAH is an angel who in the modern world oversees the safe construction and flight of aircraft and safety at air and ferry ports.

GIFTS: The potential for frequent and fulfilling travel, and to stay or live in other lands and embrace their cultures.

STRENGTHS: Good for any long-distance travel or to apply for jobs abroad.

Weaknesses: Wanderlust dreams need to be put into motion or accepted as dreams.

February 15–18

Manakiel or Manakel is the protector of sea creatures, clean seas, and the preservation of fish stocks.

Gifts: A strong affinity with water and the ability to understand what lies beneath the surface of life and people's words.

Strengths: Trust your heart and your emotions to reach out for happiness.

Weaknesses: Avoid drama kings or queens and being emotionally pressured.

February 19–24

Eiael rules spiritual studies, alternative health and spirituality, longevity, and good health.

Gifts: Talents in alternative or ancient spiritual arts, and the ability to heal through channelling angelic or other higher spiritual energies.

Strengths: Trust your intuition to find out what is really happening.

Weaknesses: Someone is out to mislead you. Ignore warnings, as you are on track.

February 25–28

Habuiah rules abundance and fertility of the land, animals, and people.

Gifts: The ability to create a fulfilling life and to welcome each life stage.

Strengths: Take a chance for an immediate source of income or gain.

Weaknesses: A bad mood or need for reassurance should be resisted.

March 1–5

ROCHEL finds lost people, animals, and birds and can be invoked for the return of lost or stolen property.

GIFTS: A leaning towards detective or security work, but more widely a strong homing instinct and psychic ability to find the right people and places throughout life.

STRENGTHS: A time for secrets to be revealed and previously silent people to speak out.

WEAKNESSES: Do not lie about your qualifications, experience, or expertise.

March 6–10

GABAMIAH blesses sacred chanting, song, and music, and those who perform, write, or take pleasure in it.

GIFTS: Musical talents and the power to understand through people's words and voices their true nature and hidden motives.

STRENGTHS: Harmony in your life and the chance to do what you want for a change.

WEAKNESSES: A tendency to say more than you intended; think before speaking.

March 11–15

HAIAIEL rules painters, calligraphers, sculptors, and all who create beautiful things with their hands.

GIFTS: Artistic abilities and the power to create beauty in different areas of life.

STRENGTHS: An amazingly creative period during which you may revive or develop an artistic gift.

WEAKNESSES: A pushy person will try to upset you out of jealousy.

March 16–20

MUMIAH blesses conventional medical treatments well as alternative
and spiritual healing, and can bring miracles in hopeless cases.

GIFTS: Evolved healing powers, whether through medicine, care-
giving professions, or personally, and an ability always to win
through.

STRENGTHS: Miracles do happen, and this could be the time.

WEAKNESSES: Beware simply hoping things will turn out well; you
also need to make an effort.

March 21–25

VEHUIAH, one of the highest-ranking orders of angels, the seraphim.
He answers prayers and rules the morning rays of the sun at the
spring equinox.

GIFTS: The ability to make every day a new beginning and constant
enthusiasm for new adventures.

STRENGTHS: Start something new that you had postponed.

WEAKNESSES: Avoid trying to change prejudiced people or en-
trenched attitudes.

March 26–30

JELIEL, another seraph, works to ensure rulers and high officials act
justly. Angel of faithful married love.

GIFTS: Ability to inspire loyalty in others and a strong social
conscience.

STRENGTHS: Increasing commitment in love or improving a marriage.

WEAKNESSES: If committed, not a day to flirt and get away with it.

March 31–April 4

SITAEL helps in times of hardship and helps those who work hard to
gain prosperity to share with others.

GIFTS: Making money, a generous nature.

STRENGTHS: Money-making ventures.

WEAKNESSES: Avoid trying to get out of paying your fair share or hiding a monetary gain.

April 5–9

ELEMIAH, a seraph who protects travellers, especially by sea, and in the modern world against road rage and traffic accidents.

GIFTS: Happy travel throughout life, and seeing beyond the immediate environment to live in different places.

STRENGTHS: Travel plans or an unexpected chance to get out of the office.

WEAKNESSES: A bad day to start work after a holiday.

April 10–14

MAHASIAH, an angel of mysteries who bears one of the secret names of God, reveals secrets and clears confusion.

GIFTS: Talents unfolding through life, intuition.

STRENGTHS: Revive an old interest or dream and join a class or society.

WEAKNESSES: Avoid tying yourself down to future commitments you are unsure about.

April 15–20

LELAHEL rules over love, both family and romantic, art in all forms, science, technology, and good luck.

GIFTS: Being in the right place at the right time, an enquiring mind.

STRENGTHS: A lucky day for love or family matters and asking someone out on a first date.

WEAKNESSES: A bad day to end a relationship or deter someone who wants to commit when you do not.

April 21–25

ACHAIAH, a seraph who knows the secrets of nature and will reveal
them to those who listen in quiet beautiful places; also an angel
of patience.

GIFTS: A love of nature and the ability to find peace and stillness,
even in a stressful environment.

STRENGTHS: Take five minutes or even the day off. Get out into the
country or the garden if possible.

WEAKNESSES: A bad day for tight deadlines or working under pressure.

April 26–30

CATHAREL, angel of gardens, crops, abundance, and fertility.

GIFTS: Self-sufficiency and the ability to create opportunities for
abundance.

STRENGTHS: Work on longer-term plans.

WEAKNESSES: Do not go on a shopping spree.

May 1–5

HAZIEL, a cherub, the second-highest order of angels, brings light
into the darkness, whether the dark nights of winter or emotional
despair.

GIFTS: Optimism, making others feel better by being in your presence.

STRENGTHS: Hang in there and share worries with others for a change.

WEAKNESSES: Avoid agonising over long-term problems or handing
in your notice.

May 6–10

ALADIAH brings stability, calms excess emotions, and turns negativity
into positive rays.

GIFTS: Peace-bringing and being a creator of joy.

STRENGTHS: Meetings, negotiations, and turning matters around.

WEAKNESSES: Avoid unnecessary confrontations.

May 11–15

LAUVIAH rules those who are naturally talented and helps them to develop unique potential and worldviews.

GIFTS: Possessing original talents, standing out from the crowd.

STRENGTHS: Launch that totally wild but winning idea.

WEAKNESSES: Avoid routine tasks or situations where you need to keep a low profile.

May 16–21

HAHAIAH, a cherub, helps preserve traditions and reveals the hidden wisdom of lost worlds to mortals.

GIFTS: Preserving tradition, passing wisdom on to others.

STRENGTHS: Maintain the status quo, contact older relatives.

WEAKNESSES: Avoid arguing with authority.

May 22–25

IEHALEL has dominion over justice and acts as an advocate for those who are unjustly accused or who live under repressive regimes.

GIFTS: Fair-mindedness, being a lifelong campaigner for justice and equality.

STRENGTHS: Tackle a minor injustice.

WEAKNESSES: Avoid one-upmanship or dubious short cuts.

May 26–31

MEBAHEL rules the distribution of wealth and assists those who cannot find work or who suffer financial hardship because of disability or illness.

GIFTS: Overcoming obstacles in your path and succeeding in spite of earlier setbacks.

STRENGTHS: Knock again on a door of opportunity previously closed; good for job hunting.

WEAKNESSES: Avoid being over-assertive, even if you are right.

June 1–5

HARIEL, angel of pets, horses, and tame creatures, protects animals against cruelty or exploitation.

GIFTS: Communication with and healing of animals, deep affinity with the animal kingdom.

STRENGTHS: Spend extra time with your pet or visit an animal park.

WEAKNESSES: Today, animals are better company than people.

June 6–10

HAKAMIAH, a cherub who guards against treachery, false friends, and unwise investments or contracts.

GIFTS: Discernment and the power to discriminate between what is true and of worth from what is false or illusory.

STRENGTHS: Follow the safe option; read the small print twice.

WEAKNESSES: Avoid special offers, sales, or Internet bargains.

June 11–15

LAUVIAH encourages all who seek to communicate their gifts whether through writing, inventions, or technological skills.

GIFTS: Writing, computers, and communication skills.

STRENGTHS: Start your novel or create the computer game that will make a million.

WEAKNESSES: Avoid people who talk in circles and have no intention of delivering.

June 16–21

CALIEL, from the order of Thrones, the cosmic traveller, aids all who are in perilous places or situations or who live in communities where security is a problem.

GIFTS: Protection throughout life from danger and the ability to win the trust of others, personally and professionally.

STRENGTHS: Persuade others to see and do things your way.

WEAKNESSES: Check domestic security systems and personal safety to avoid unnecessary risks.

June 22–26

LEUVIAH rules hidden knowledge, and helps to avoid intrusion in our lives as well as those who would steal credit for our ideas.

GIFTS: Independence from the need for the approval of others; self-reliance.

STRENGTHS: Tell an interfering person to back off. Good for independent enterprises.

WEAKNESSES: Avoid emotional vampires and angst-ridden people.

June 27–July 1

PAHALIAH spreads faith to unbelievers and encourages high standards of conduct.

GIFTS: Integrity, brings spiritual values into everyday living

STRENGTHS: Take some self-time and switch off mobile phones and leave the computer whenever possible.

WEAKNESSES: Beware of being too honest as you may soon regret it.

July 2–July 6

NELCHAEL, an angel of the Thrones, teaches astronomy and mathematics, and encourages ecological awareness and responsibility.

GIFTS: Innate environmental awareness, a thirst for knowledge, especially of other places and lifestyles.

STRENGTHS: Go all-out for a more environmentally friendly workplace and neighbourhood.

WEAKNESSES: Avoid pollution, stress, and noise.

July 7–11

YEIAYEL protects and brings loving warmth to the home and family, and ensures that absent members keep in touch.

GIFTS: The ability to feel and make others feel at home.

STRENGTHS: Go home early and spend an evening with family or alone.

WEAKNESSES: Avoid confrontation with critical relatives and difficult neighbours.

July 12–16

MEHALEL, another mystical angel, draws a veil over past losses and betrayal and uplifts us with promises of a better tomorrow.

GIFTS: The power to make the best of any situation; transforming a potential disaster into triumph.

STRENGTHS: Look for the silver lining and keep smiling; a small home improvement will work wonders.

WEAKNESSES: Avoid saying never or closing doors.

July 17–22

HAHUEUIAH, whose name means "service to others," encourages respect for traditional values and the wisdom of older people.

GIFTS: Having a natural gift with older people and an instinctive understanding of ancient wisdom; being an old soul from birth.

STRENGTHS: Take the advice of an older or wiser friend or colleague.

WEAKNESSES: Watch out for doom and gloom merchants and believing their words.

July 23–27

NITHAIAH is the angel of poets from the angelic order of Dominions, the angels responsible for major miracles. He is an angel of prophecy and protects peacemakers.

GIFTS: Talent with the written and spoken word and the ability to heal through kind words and the power of the voice.

STRENGTHS: Speak from your heart and you will resolve a misunderstanding.

WEAKNESSES: Avoid asking for opinions you may not want to hear.

July 28–August 1

HAAIAH, another Dominions angel, whose special role is over diplomacy, seeks to soften the hearts of dictators and reduce warmongering and greed.

GIFTS: A natural negotiator and diplomat with the ability to melt hearts and change stubborn viewpoints.

STRENGTHS: Ask for a salary increase or promotion, or apply for other jobs.

WEAKNESSES: Make sure the person you are defending is worth it.

August 2–6

YERATEL, another Dominions angel, is a light bringer and protects those imprisoned unfairly, especially far from home.

GIFTS: A free spirit for whom quality of life and happiness will always be more important than material possessions.

STRENGTHS: A time to do something spontaneous and fun.

WEAKNESSES: Avoid throwing everything up on a whim.

August 7–12

SEHEIAH protects against accidents, disease, illness, and natural disasters.

GIFTS: Good health, long life, and protection from life's natural hazards.

STRENGTHS: Lady Luck is with you, so a good day for entering a competition.

WEAKNESSES: Avoid overindulgence, as your body will not respond well.

August 13–17

REIIEL, an angel of Dominions, encourages idealism and works towards fair elections of leaders everywhere.

GIFTS: Idealism, altruism, and a natural tendency towards leadership that may not emerge until later in life.

STRENGTHS: Apply for promotion or take the initiative.

WEAKNESSES: Avoid promising what you cannot deliver.

August 18–23

OMAEL brings fertility to all the species on the earth and encourages diversity of languages and cultures.

GIFTS: An ability to learn different languages, embrace different lifestyles, and creativity that increases with age.

STRENGTHS: Good for overseas dealings or signing up for a language course.

WEAKNESSES: Avoid spreading yourself too thinly.

August 24–28

LECABEL rules over vegetation, growth of crops, and agricultural workers, and keeps food natural and pure.

GIFTS: Growing achievements through life, harmony with your own bodily rhythms, the cycles of the natural world, and the seasons.

STRENGTHS: Starting any diet, exercise, or fitness regimes.

WEAKNESSES: Avoid overempathising with the problems of others.

August 29–September 2

VASAIRIAH rules justice, the legal system, and all those who administer justice in courts, especially for environmental, domestic, and civil rights.

GIFTS: A highly evolved sense of right and wrong and a natural mind for understanding the intricacies of justice and the law.

STRENGTHS: Good for legal matters; also good for buying, selling, or renting property.

WEAKNESSES: Watch out for pettiness and behavior police.

September 3–7

YEHUDIAH is present at the beginning of life and gently carries souls at the end of life to the afterlife.

GIFTS: Being a natural healer and, in later life, mediumship and clairvoyancy.

STRENGTHS: Letting go of what has run its course.

WEAKNESSES: Fretting over what you cannot have and missing what is up for the taking.

September 8–12

LEHAHIAH, from the angelic order of Powers, the cosmic police force, who encourages the need for fair government and wise laws.

GIFTS: The ability to accept life's rules but to question the status quo when necessary; a sense of true morality.

STRENGTHS: Good for official matters, planning applications, for signing home or job contracts.

WEAKNESSES: Ignoring official paperwork and final demands.

September 13–17

CHAVAQUIAH encourages stillness and contemplation and so is a good angel in a frantic, modern world.

GIFTS: The ability to live and thrive within the everyday world but not to be overwhelmed by it.

STRENGTHS: Pace yourself and renegotiate impossible deadlines and demands.

WEAKNESSES: Avoid taking on the panic, stress, and hyperactivity induced by others.

September 18–22

MENADEL, of the order of Powers, blesses all who are far from their native land.

GIFTS: The ability to maintain loving connections with others regardless of distance, and to become part of the global family.

STRENGTHS: Good for contacting people whom you wish were still a part of your life.

WEAKNESSES: Making excuses rather than admitting a relationship or friendship is best consigned to memory.

September 23–28

ANIEL guards the gates of the home of the West Wind and brings comfort to older people and those of any age who are disabled or chronically unwell.

GIFTS: Being a natural healer and a carer for all in distress, and a good friend who will enjoy lasting friendships in return.

STRENGTHS: Make time for friendships and for face-to-face communication.

WEAKNESSES: Do not put work demands before friends and family.

September 29–October 3

HAAIMIAH, an angel of the Powers, encourages peaceful coexistence of different faiths, tolerance, and personal honesty.

GIFTS: Tolerance, acceptance, and understanding of differences in others and an honesty that inspires trust and respect.

STRENGTHS: Forgive old grudges and do not harp on others' failings.

WEAKNESSES: Be careful not to be blamed for the mistakes of others.

October 4–8

REHAEL, an angel of the Powers, brings good health and long life, and helps those in parenting roles.

GIFTS: Being a natural teacher, especially of the young, and the assurance of long and a healthy life ahead.

STRENGTHS: Spend time with children or let your inner child out to play.

WEAKNESSES: Avoid serious discussions.

October 9–13

IHIAZEL rules negotiations between individuals, family factions, workplace disputes, groups, or nations.

GIFTS: Ability to mend quarrels and to attract a wide and fruitful social life.

STRENGTHS: Arrange a social event soon and see difficult family members.

WEAKNESSES: Do not be a doormat.

October 14–18

HAHAHEL, from the angelic order of Virtues, brings small miracles and peace. He watches over aid and charity workers and carers at home and abroad.

GIFTS: Being a natural giver to others, a force for good in the world, and someone who takes responsibility for the planet's well-being.

STRENGTHS: Sort out your own home life, so you are living where and how you want.

WEAKNESSES: Watch out for someone taking your ideas, your wallet, or your heart.

October 19–23

MIKAEL banishes corruption in official bodies, organisations, and companies, and helps all in positions of authority to be impartial.

GIFTS: Becoming a seeker of truth and inspiring high standards of conduct in others.

STRENGTHS: Trust what people are saying. Good for loans, mortgages, or financial dealings.

WEAKNESSES: Not a time to ring in sick or invent a distant relative's funeral.

October 24–28

VEULIAH, from the angelic order of Principalities, oversees life changes and softens stubborn or destructive attitudes in others.

GIFTS: A totally open attitude to life and its changes; the ability to persuade others and influence them for the better.

STRENGTHS: Right now you could sell ice cubes to the frozen north, so be proactive.

WEAKNESSES: Avoid yard sales or bargain hunting.

October 29–November 2

YELAIAH rules inspiration and starlight and brings the fulfilment of realistic dreams.

GIFTS: Being one of life's dreamers and visionaries, inspiring others and bringing dreams into reality.

STRENGTHS: A time to pull off what seemed impossible last week.

WEAKNESSES: Remember to get out of bed.

November 3–7

SAHALIAH, one of the order of Virtues, who rules the harvest, and encourages organic and humane farming methods.

GIFTS: The ability to make every day like a celebration, and making others feel welcome and cared for.

STRENGTHS: Throw an impromptu party or invite people home for a potluck meal.

WEAKNESSES: An unexpected visitor may outstay their welcome.

November 8–12

ARIEL, the archangel of nature and wildlife, rules the waters and the winds. He transforms sickness into health and exhaustion into energy.

GIFTS: The ability to heal people, animals, and places with natural methods and to radiate enthusiasm, energy, and happiness.

STRENGTHS: A good time to take up a healing art or environmental cause.

WEAKNESSES: Watch out for lame ducks quacking up to your desk or door.

November 13–17

ASALIAH, who comes from the order of Virtues, puts right injustice while diminishing a desire for vengeance or retribution.

GIFTS: A powerful but healing presence in any walk of life, and the ability to find good in any situation or person.

STRENGTHS: You will discover unexpected allies and see the better side of someone you dislike.

WEAKNESSES: Do not accept disrespectful behaviour, even jokingly.

November 18–22

MIHAEL, from the order of Virtues, rules married love, fidelity, and the safety of newborn children and their mothers.

GIFTS: Happiness in love and a natural affinity to mothers, babies and motherhood, whether personally or professionally.

STRENGTHS: Good for conception, parenting, or for contacting your parents.

WEAKNESSES: Who said you had to mother helpless, lazy adults?

November 23–27

VEHUEL, a Principalities angel, encourages original, creative thinking and the teaching of new ideas to stimulate the minds of the young.

GIFTS: Literary gifts and the ability to teach others.

STRENGTHS: Start that book we all have within us, or begin a diary.

WEAKNESSES: Do not give away ideas to people who will claim credit for them.

November 28–December 2

DANIEL, Principalities angel, rules accountants, taxation, and legal officials, so that they will exercise high standards of honesty and fairness.

GIFTS: The ability to bring order to chaos, accuracy, seeing patterns and structures in seemingly random events.

STRENGTHS: A day to use feng shui on your paperwork, tax returns, and irritating forms.

WEAKNESSES: You did not create the problem, so do not clear it up.

December 3–7

HAHAZIAH expands the spiritual potential of individuals, as well as bringing a more spiritual focus into family life and society generally.

GIFTS: Spiritual understanding to enrich everyday life or to follow a spiritual path.

STRENGTHS: Step back and ask where you are going, and why.

WEAKNESSES: Avoid well-meaning amateur gurus.

December 8–12

IMAMIAH, a Principalities angel, assists all who travel, especially commuters and those journeying long distances.

GIFTS: To be one of life's travellers with the ability to break through restrictions and not be limited in the scope of your actual or mental discoveries.

STRENGTHS: Good for actual journeys or to join new online networking groups.

WEAKNESSES: Sort out what you need to do urgently closer to home.

December 13–16

NANAEL, another angel of Principalities, rules scholarship, science, philosophy, and religion, and helps those with learning difficulties.

GIFTS: Teaching abilities beyond the conventional to bring enlightenment to any who struggle; clarity of vision to discriminate between fact and fiction.

STRENGTHS: Good for running seminars and attending or organising courses.

WEAKNESSES: Check if what you are told is fact or fiction.

December 17–21

NITHAEL, also of the Principalities, rules international bodies such as NATO and the United Nations.

GIFTS: An ability to see the bigger picture and lead others to become more adventurous and see possibilities beyond their immediate environment.

STRENGTHS: A good time to assess if the roles you occupy towards others are ones you want or were imposed through duty or guilt.

WEAKNESSES: Check e-mails or work carefully as you may have missed a vital detail or made a mistake.

December 22–26

MEBAHIAH rules fertility and helps those who want children but are having difficulties conceiving. He is also an angel of conscience.

GIFTS: Bearing and bringing of fertility in its widest meaning and always acting from the best motives.

STRENGTHS: Good for fertility matters, especially tests or treatment.

WEAKNESSES: Do not waste time on a project that is not working out.

December 27–31

POIEL, a Principalities angel, is guardian of the future we have yet to make and is active in assisting us to make wise choices about that future.

GIFTS: Natural clairvoyance and the ability to use it to plan ahead and advise others.

STRENGTHS: Good for career appraisal and exploring options.

WEAKNESSES: Sit tight for a few days and keep your doubts to yourself.

Day Angels and Relationships

Birthday angels explain why certain people have character strengths and why you instantly get on with some people and not others. If you know a person's birthday angel, you will better understand them. When you know what matters to a person, you can subtly alter your approach to avoid any hot spots and focus on their strengths.

For example, if you have a new manager or colleague born between 1–5 March, Rochel, their birthday angel, gives them a natural tendency to seek out the truth and an almost uncanny knack to read people. Thus, there is no point in exaggerating your qualifications or past achievements as they will respect an upfront approach and realistic assessment of what you can and cannot offer.

The Archangel Hours

Archangel hours are remarkably useful in your daily life. Below is a modern and increasingly popular way of calculating the angel hours, which applies to wherever you live in the world. Using this information you can assess the best time of day or night to contact someone. For instance, if you have an important phone call to make, choose an hour that is angelically favourable for the purpose. Perhaps you want to make a family call or send an e-mail to a lover—if so, you would choose an hour when Anael, the archangel of love and families, rules. The appropriate hour on an archangel's day of the week (see overleaf) makes any request or ritual doubly effective, so the two Anael hours on a Friday would be a good time.

Midnight to midday (00:00–11:59)
and midday to midnight (12:00–23:59)

Hours	Sun	Mon	Tues	Wed	Thurs	Fri	Sat
0:00–0:59	Michael	Gabriel	Samael	Raphael	Sachiel	Anael	Cassiel
1:00–1:59	Anael	Cassiel	Michael	Gabriel	Samael	Raphael	Sachiel
2:00–2:59	Raphael	Sachiel	Anael	Cassiel	Michael	Gabriel	Samael
3:00–3:59	Gabriel	Samael	Raphael	Sachiel	Anael	Cassiel	Michael
4:00–4:59	Cassiel	Michael	Gabriel	Samael	Raphael	Sachiel	Anael
5:00–5:59	Sachiel	Anael	Cassiel	Michael	Gabriel	Samael	Raphael
6:00–6:59	Samael	Raphael	Sachiel	Anael	Cassiel	Michael	Gabriel
7:00–7:59	Michael	Gabriel	Samael	Raphael	Sachiel	Anael	Cassiel
8:00–8:59	Anael	Cassiel	Michael	Gabriel	Samael	Raphael	Sachiel
9:00–9:59	Raphael	Sachiel	Anael	Cassiel	Michael	Gabriel	Samael
10:00–10:59	Gabriel	Samael	Raphael	Sachiel	Anael	Cassiel	Michael
11:00–11:59	Cassiel	Michael	Gabriel	Samael	Raphael	Sachiel	Anael
12:00–12:59	Sachiel	Anael	Cassiel	Michael	Gabriel	Samael	Raphael
13:00–13:59	Samael	Raphael	Sachiel	Anael	Cassiel	Michael	Gabriel
14:00–14:59	Michael	Gabriel	Samael	Raphael	Sachiel	Anael	Cassiel
15:00–15:59	Anael	Cassiel	Michael	Gabriel	Samael	Raphael	Sachiel
16:00–16:59	Raphael	Sachiel	Anael	Cassiel	Michael	Gabriel	Samael
17:00–17:59	Gabriel	Samael	Raphael	Sachiel	Anael	Cassiel	Michael
18:00–18:59	Cassiel	Michael	Gabriel	Samael	Raphael	Sachiel	Anael
19:00–19:59	Sachiel	Anael	Cassiel	Michael	Gabriel	Samael	Raphael
20:00–20:59	Samael	Raphael	Sachiel	Anael	Cassiel	Michael	Gabriel
21:00–21:59	Michael	Gabriel	Samael	Raphael	Sachiel	Anael	Cassiel
22:00–22:59	Anael	Cassiel	Michael	Gabriel	Samael	Raphael	Sachiel
23:00–23:59	Raphael	Sachiel	Anael	Cassiel	Michael	Gabriel	Samael

To work with the angel hours of another time zone, calculate what time it will be where the person you are contacting lives and choose that hour from the chart above. The time of sending or contact is crucial, even if they do not pick up the message until later.

The Days of the Week

The different days of the week are also ruled by the seven archangels. A combination of the right day and the corresponding angel hours of the day will give you a strong enough boost to counteract any unfavourable moon or zodiac periods for different ventures. The more angelic aspects that harmonise, the more easily things will flow. You will learn more of the seven archangels in chapter 9.

The archangels have their own special colours, crystals, and fragrances. If possible, before beginning any contact, light a candle and fragrance whose energies represent that archangel. You can also hold their crystal as you ask the angel for help.

Sunday ☉

ARCHANGEL: Michael, who rules the sun

PLANET: Sun

ELEMENT: Fire

COLOURS: Gold, orange

CRYSTALS: Amber, carnelian, clear crystal quartz, diamond, tiger's eye, topaz

INCENSES AND OILS: Bay, cinnamon, chamomile, copal (plant or tree resin), frankincense, juniper, orange, rosemary

METAL: Gold

Use the energies of Michael and Sunday for personal fulfilment and ambition; power and success; fathers and mature men; new beginnings; creative energy; joy; improving health, prosperity, and self-confidence; and overcoming bad luck.

Monday ☽

ARCHANGEL: Gabriel, who rules the moon

PLANET: Moon

ELEMENT: Water

COLOUR: Silver

CRYSTALS: Moonstone, mother-of-pearl, opal, pearl, selenite
INCENSES AND OILS: Eucalyptus, jasmine, lemon, lotus, myrrh, poppy
METAL: Silver

Use the energies of Gabriel and Monday for home and family matters; for all women's needs and problems, especially mothers and grandmothers, children, and animals; fertility; protection, especially while travelling; for clairvoyance and psychic dreams; for healing; and for keeping secrets and discovering what others are hiding.

Tuesday ♂

ARCHANGEL: Samael, the angel of cleansing fire and of courage
PLANET: Mars
ELEMENT: Fire
COLOUR: Red
CRYSTALS: Bloodstone, garnet, jasper, ruby
INCENSE AND OILS: Cypress, dragon's blood, ginger and all spices, heather, hibiscus, mint, pine, tarragon, thyme
METAL: Iron, steel

Use the energies of Samael and Tuesday for courage, change, taking the initiative, independence, resisting injustice; protection from bullying, gossip, spite, malice, and lies; for overcoming seemingly impossible odds; for health and vitality; for passion, the consummation of love; for matters concerning young men, and for all in the armed forces or security services.

Wednesday ☿

ARCHANGEL: Raphael, the traveller and healer
PLANET: Mercury
ELEMENT: Air
COLOUR: Yellow
CRYSTALS: Any agate, ametrine, citrine, falcon's eye, malachite, onyx white sapphire, yellow jasper

INCENSES AND OILS: Lavender, lemon balm, lemon grass, lily of the valley

METAL: Platinum

Use the energies of Raphael and Wednesday for money-making ventures, clear communication, persuasion, adaptability, versatility, improving memory, and sharpening logic; for teenagers; for study and examinations; for mastering new technology; for short-distance travel, house moves, or short-break holidays; for conventional methods of healing, especially surgery; for business negotiations; for overcoming debt; and for repelling envy, malice, spite, and deceit.

Thursday ♃

ARCHANGEL: Sachiel, who rules the harvest and abundance

PLANET: Jupiter

ELEMENT: Air

COLOURS: Blue, purple

CRYSTALS: Azurite, blue sapphire, chrysocolla, lapis lazuli, sodalite, turquoise

INCENSES AND OILS: Cedar, clove, honeysuckle, sage, sandalwood

METALS: Bronze, tin

Use the energies of Sachiel and Thursday for expansion, career, leadership, learned wisdom, long-distance travel, house moves, justice and the law, authority, marriage, permanent relationships, business partnerships, middle-aged people, fidelity, loyalty, male potency, and for banishing excesses and addictions.

Friday ♀

ARCHANGEL: Anael, who rules love, fidelity and all matters of steady increase or growth

PLANET: Venus

ELEMENT: Earth

COLOURS: Green, pink

CRYSTALS: Amethyst, emerald, jade, moss agate, rose quartz

INCENSES AND OILS: Apple blossom, geranium, lemon verbena, lilac, lily and lily of the valley, rose, strawberry

METAL: Copper

Use the energies of Anael and Friday for love, relationships, and friendships; for young women; for beauty and arts and crafts; marriage and fidelity; blossoming sexuality; the acquisition of beautiful possessions; mending quarrels, peace, the environment, fertility and women's health matters; for gradual growth and improvement; also for reducing the influence of destructive lovers, and possessiveness.

Saturday ♄

ARCHANGEL: Cassiel, who rules compassion and assists us to cope within the limits of reality and current restrictions. He also helps us find ways around those restrictions and expand our horizons.

PLANET: Saturn

ELEMENT: Earth

COLOURS: Black, brown, grey

CRYSTALS: Fossils, hematite, jet, lodestone, obsidian, turitella agate, smoky quartz

INCENSE: Carnation, cypress, mimosa, pansy, patchouli, tea tree

METAL: Pewter

Use the energies of Cassiel and Saturday for resolving unfinished business, accepting endings that lead to beginnings; for slow-moving matters and working within limitations; overcoming long-standing obstacles; easing depression or doubts; official matters; for psychic protection and binding spells; animals and older people; locating lost objects; regaining self-control over bad habits or emotions; repayment of money owed; and banishing pain, guilt, or illness.

Putting it all together

With such a wonderful array of angelic influences to work with, you can generally find a day or time when at least two kinds of angelic energies are working with you. Spend an hour or two any evening towards the end of each month creating a chart for the month ahead, marking the angels who are around on prearranged appointments or events you cannot change. If necessary, see if you can reorganise your schedule to when the moon angel is associated by the zodiac angel in one of those precious two and a half day periods each month. If not, skim though the lists to find an ideal angel whose day- or five-day period is close by and ask for assistance from the angels who are around on a particular day.

For each five-day period, note the potential strengths and pitfalls so you are forewarned. If there is a special event like a wedding or a date, look at your birthday angels and those of the other person. See how they mesh and how by adjusting dates and times you can add mitigating energies. Remember, you can use the colours, crystals, and fragrances of the ruling zodiac angel to connect with the angel of a particular five-day period.

The planning process is worthwhile. You will find stresses become less, obstacles more negotiable, and people generally more receptive.

If in doubt, ask your guardian angel to connect you to the right angels. Relax and enjoy even the potentially most stressful week.

nine

ANGELIC PROTECTION
AND INSPIRATION

When I was a little girl, I always asked the angels to protect me while I slept, as I was terrified of the dark. In adulthood, we generally cope with what life offers or, on occasions, throws at us. Yet however supercompetent we are, there are times—such as a sudden crisis, feeling vulnerable after an illness, or when facing the uncertainties of travel in a potentially dangerous world—that we do feel the need for protection. To angels, whether we are the president of a major corporation or have climbed Everest, we are no different from the small child who is scared when the light is turned out. You need never feel stupid, inadequate, or incompetent when you call on angels for help, for there are times when we all feel vulnerable and need to sense we are cherished and will be kept safe.

The following are just two examples of how angels have protected people at major crisis points in their lives.

A LITTLE GIRL'S ANGELIC RESCUE
IN A TRAFFIC ACCIDENT

Debbie was waiting to see her young daughter across the street to catch the school bus. An oncoming car on the northbound lane side had stopped, and as no traffic was coming in the southbound lane, the little girl crossed. However, a car behind the stationary vehicle was coming up much too fast. The driver swerved out into the southbound lane and sped towards Debbie's daughter, now in the middle of the road.

Yet just as suddenly, the car swerved round the child and back into the correct lane, with the precision of what Debbie called "a highly skilled Formula 1 driver." The car driver had a long thin nose, a long thin face framed by chin length, straight silvery blonde hair and brilliant blue eyes. Debbie described the woman in the police report that she filed later that morning.

When the case came to court, the driver, a woman with a very round face, round nose, brown eyes, and curly brown hair, pleaded guilty to speeding. At that moment Debbie *knew* the reassuring face that had looked straight into her eyes that morning was the face of an angel as it had saved her little girl's life.

ANGELIC PROTECTION FROM THIEVES

Katrena was in the back room of a shop, which she used as a consulting room for her work as a spiritual practitioner. She suddenly heard the strained voice of Val, who was working behind the counter. As Katrena entered the shop, she saw a young man standing at the door, holding it open. Another man near the counter was talking very fast and low to Val. Katrena realised that these men were about to rob the shop. She asked her angels for protection.

At that moment, the younger man at the door looked at Katrena with a startled expression, gasped, and fled out of the door. The older man also looked at her, baffled, and immediately followed.

Angel Charms for Protection

Some people use a small glass, silver, or crystal angel charm as inspiration and for protection. Carry one in a small purse, wear one as a pendant on a chain (you can buy tiny pendant crystal angels), or put one in the glove box of the car to keep you safe. I hold my glove-box angel for a minute or two when I take a break at a service area while driving on a long journey by car (I am not a confident driver) and also when I travel by plane as we come into land (which I hate).

JANICE'S TWO ANGELS OF PROTECTION

Janice, who lives in New Zealand, told Leela, the editor of the Australian magazine *Spheres*, that her mother gave her two crystal angels for protection, one for the house and one for the car. While driving four weeks later, Janice was caught in a horrendous storm during which the local barn collapsed, scattering debris and blocking the road. When Janice was finally able to reach home, still with iron and wood blowing all round her, she discovered that not only had there been no damage to the house in the chaos, but no wood or corrugated iron had fallen on the ground near the house at all. Yet at the other side of the property, pine trees had blown down.

That night, once power returned, Janice noticed the house lights getting rapidly brighter. In the morning, she discovered that two of the surge-protector plugs had melted. Janice went into the shower, which had a metal base. Suddenly the bathroom lights became like floodlights and she received an electric shock as she put the shower back in its holder, followed by an even bigger shock when she touched the taps. When the emergency power workers came, they discovered there was no ground to the mains because of a wire that had come down in the storm. As Janice's house was the last on the road, she had been getting the full undiluted power of the rest of the houses through her system.

Janice is convinced her crystal angels gave her protection to cheat potential death three times, once from the falling debris, trees, and collapsing barn on the car journey, once from the power surges that could have set fire to the house while she slept, and thirdly, from electrocution in the shower.

Angelic Inspiration

Seemingly inexplicable signs can offer us reassurance that the angels are with us in times of doubt. John and Anne, who had recently retired, were moving to a rented house in Shropshire, having been staying with their son after selling their own house some months earlier. They had no idea where they would live longterm and had thought about Ireland or France as possibilities. As they packed their final belongings on the morning of the move, they felt very uncertain whether they were doing the right thing moving to Shropshire. The week before moving, John, Anne, and their son had been listening to *The Lord of the Rings* tapes in the evenings and had been struck by the phrase "May you find a fair haven," which became a catchphrase for them.

Just as the moving van drew up at 7:30 AM, an unsigned card dropped through the door saying, *"You will find a fair haven."* Anne and John were happy in Shropshire and eventually moved to France. The picture on the card resembles the area they now live, which is not at all where they had expected to move. They still have the card and have a new lease on life, running a very successful bed and breakfast business. Anne has returned to painting and has sold her work in local exhibitions.

Creating an angel sanctuary for inspiration

Some people create an outdoor angel sanctuary where they go for daily inspiration, if only for five minutes. Such a sanctuary is easy to make, even in the smallest outdoor space or a corner of a balcony.

You can plant zodiac or archangel flowers or herbs, arrange crystals, and buy a stone angel for the centre. On the other hand, you may know of a natural rock formation not too far from home where one of the rocks resembles a kneeling angel.

Vanda, from South Wales, described her sanctuary: "I have created a sacred place in my garden, which is made of natural rock. It has a water feature and a large stone angel. I am planning to set crystals around the four corners of my sacred place to keep it protected and give it celestial energy—amethyst or citrine in the east for the air angels, rose quartz in the north for the earth angels, carnelian in the south for the fire angels and jade in the west for the water angels. I often burn candles there and meditate or talk with my angels, and I give my sacred place Reiki and through it, via the angels, I give Reiki to the universe."

Angelic inspiration and children

Children have no problem seeing angels everywhere and drawing inspiration from them, but for adults, especially very logical people, it can be harder to tune into this source of wisdom that can remind us, especially in hard times, that there is more to life than the material world. As Tina, who lives in Wales, explained, sometimes it takes a child to show us an angel when we, the adults, may be looking in entirely the wrong place.

HANNAH'S ANGEL

When Tina's daughter Hannah was nine, they visited St. Michael's Mount. Hannah was given a quiz to complete on the tour of the castle and grounds.

One of the questions on the quiz sheet was about the location of the monument where St. Michael first appeared on the island. Suddenly, Hannah stopped and pointed out a plain grey rock sticking out. She described a humanlike form kneeling, with hair glowing golden and wings folded at the back, pointing down. Her angel was looking down at the ground and almost blended into the grey of the rock. Hannah was getting frustrated because her mother could not see the angel. As they walked away, Hannah would not stop looking back at the rock. When Tina and Hannah reached the monument marked on the map where St. Michael was said to have appeared, Tina pointed it out, but Hannah was adamant that this was not the place and the guide book had it wrong. Years later, Hannah still insists she saw the angel, and her mother believes her. Tina also says Hannah has a wonderful healing energy.

Working with the archangels for inspiration

For protection and inspiration, we can consult the archangels for those times when we need a bit of extra input. You have been introduced to several archangels such as Michael and Chamuel in previous chapters, but here we will work with even more of the traditional archangels. I have added extra information about those you have already encountered.

You can contact the archangels for protection or inspiration by creating angel blessings or by using one of the oldest techniques in angel spirituality: writing a letter.

Creating an angel blessing

There is no purpose too trivial or too great to ask for a blessing for yourself or someone else. Write the blessing out on good-quality paper in the coloured ink I have suggested in the archangel list on pages 192–205, and tie it in a scroll with the appropriately coloured ribbon. Either send it to the intended recipient or, if for yourself, keep it in your angel space and read it regularly.

If you think the intended recipient might feel uncomfortable receiving a blessing, you can keep their scroll in your angel place, light the appropriate candles, and say the words as if they were speaking.

You can easily create your own blessing using the format below for any inspirational or protective purpose:

1. DEFINE THE PURPOSE OF THE BLESSING

2. CHOOSE THE ARCHANGEL OR ANGELS WHO CAN HELP

To send a blessing for a newborn child or on an anniversary, you would include the relevant month, zodiac angel and birthday angel and associated colours, etc. (see pages 138–141). For a wedding or anniversary, you would work with the angel of day the event was planned plus the zodiac, birthday, and month angels of the couple involved.

3. DESCRIBE THE ARCHANGEL OR ANGEL

This is so you can picture in your mind the source of help or assist the person to whom you are sending the blessing to imagine the angel. Write down the role of the angel and describe the appearance using the lists on pages 192–205 or the earlier zodiac angel descriptions. If you are using a birthday angel, close your eyes and let an image come into your mind. You could put this on a separate sheet or above the blessing on the main paper.

4. DEFINE THE BLESSING TIMINGS

Unless for a specific occasion such as a birthday or wedding, a blessing is most powerful on the archangel's own day at their particular time (see the archangel lists on pages 192–205) but it can, however, be spoken or read whenever there is a need.

There is often a time span during which particular archangel blessings are most likely to manifest. Often, within his or her time frame, the archangel will enable you to think of a practical solution or will send an earthly opportunity and maybe an unexpected piece of good luck. Therefore, you could write the following as a reminder (substituting your angels and times) on your blessing paper or the separate sheet:

> *Recite Cassiel's blessing on a Saturday evening after dark once a week for four weeks and any other occasion when you/I need good luck within this period.*

Writing the blessing

Imagine you are asking a favour of an older, slightly old-fashioned but kindly relative. This is a good way of setting the blessing just a little above the everyday world.

Use the appropriate coloured paper and ink. Sit quietly in your angel place and let the words flow. Light the main angel's candle colour and an incense stick in one of their fragrances. When you have finished, read what you have written but do not change or rewrite it unless absolutely necessary.

If you are stuck as to what to write, use this structure from my Cassiel good-luck blessing as a guideline. As a matter of course, you will need to alter the language for the angel you are entreating:

1. ADDRESS THE ANGEL

Acknowledge the strengths of the angel or angels you are calling:

> *Wise Cassiel, you who wait patiently and with understanding without judging those who find themselves in dire circumstance or troubled by misfortune.*

2. SAY WHAT YOU NEED AND WHY YOU HAVE CHOSEN THIS ANGEL

> *Benign archangel who turns the Wheel of Fortune, relieve this burden that weighs so heavily on me (specify your problem here)*

and restore good fortune to my life. Make luck smile once more on me, restoring better days ahead.

3. DETAIL THE HELP YOU NEED

Wise archangel, take away the obstacles and worries that in the night seem mountains high. If it is right to be, bring me unexpected good luck also, or a win, however modest, to boost my ailing fortunes.

4. THANK THE ARCHANGEL AND THE CLOSING

I thank you Cassiel, and wait with trust and patience for your blessings that the tide of good fortune will at last turn in my favour.

Even as you write your blessing, you may feel a sense of relief and greater confidence.

Carrying out a blessing ritual

Writing and then reading the blessing aloud is in itself a ritual and may be all you need to do. In addition, however, you or the recipient could light the archangel's candle and add one of the fragrances and crystals as suggested below. These could also be sent as a gift to the recipient. For more than one angel, mix and match the symbols to include one from each angel you are calling.

A CASSIEL RITUAL TO STRENGTHEN A GOOD-LUCK BLESSING

You can adapt this to any angel or purpose. Please note that the candle colours and scents, as well as the incense, crystals, and ribbon colours used below correspond to Cassiel. Use the correspondences in the following pages to find the appropriate materials for your angel.

1. Just before bedtime, light a burgundy or indigo candle and set a green aventurine or jade crystal and/or some dried cooking sage in a small drawstring bag or purse so the candlelight shines on it.

2. Put a single gold-coloured coin of any denomination in front of the candle.

3. Light one of the angel's fragrances, such as patchouli, as an incense stick or fragrance oil.

4. Read your blessing twice consecutively very softly, so your words almost fade into silence at the end of the second blessing.

5. Leave the incense to burn through and blow out the candle at bedtime. Carry your crystal and/or herb purse as a good-luck charm in the days ahead.

6. Tie the blessing in a scroll tied with indigo or burgundy ribbon, secured with three knots.

7. Put the coin in a pot with a lid in your special angel place or in a warm indoor spot. Each time you carry out the ritual or recite the blessing, add another coin to the pot to symbolise growing good fortune.

Though some archangels can offer results quite rapidly, for a slow-moving matter or long-term problem you may, after reciting the initial blessing several times within the time frame (specified as *Results* in the lists of archangels on pages 192–205), start another blessings cycle and continue the blessings as long as you need.

Making your own blessing rituals

By using the different symbols associated with the archangels, you can create your own mini-rituals for any purpose. The following are some suggestions:

+ Light an archangel or zodiac angel candle to begin the ritual and blow it out at the end of the blessing, to send the light symbolically into your own energy field or into those for whom you are carrying out the blessing.

+ Light an incense stick in a relevant fragrance from the candle and write in smoke over the candle the purpose of the blessing. This is a good way of releasing what may seem an unmoving situation, to attract prosperity, better health or success, or launch a creative venture.

+ Write in incense smoke the angel or archangel name(s) over an archangel crystal or piece of jewellery made of an angelic metal. This fills it with angelic power and purpose, so it acts as a good-luck talisman.

+ A bag of culinary herbs can be empowered in the same way. If you put the herbs in a plastic inner bag before adding them to the purse, you could afterwards add them to food or use to make herbal tea to absorb the angelic energies.

+ For matters of increase, each time you say the blessing add a small item such as a coin or a thin ring or earring in the angel's metal on each occasion to a lidded pot to symbolise the accumulating strengths of the blessings.

+ To remove pain, sorrow, or ill health, on each occasion add a few dried herbs or dying petals or leaves from an angel tree or flower to a bowl of soil. Scatter these to the winds, drop them in flowing water, or bury them after carrying out the blessing three or four times.

+ When you want to make a more elaborate blessing ceremony, trust yourself to ask the angels, and the right actions will come.

The Archangels

Michael

ROLE: Supreme archangel and archangel of the sun, who oversees the natural world, and the weather; leader of all the great warrior angels and traditional dragon slayer

IMAGE: Golden wings in red and gold armour with sword and shield, a green date branch, and carrying the scales of justice or a white banner with a red cross

DAY: Sunday

TIME OF DAY: Noon

COLOURS: Gold, orange

FRAGRANCES: Copal (plant or tree resin), frankincense, orange, rosemary

FLOWERS AND HERBS: Chamomile, cinnamon, marigold, sunflower

TREES AND PLANTS: Bay (laurel), date palm, juniper, orange

CRYSTALS: Amber, carnelian, diamond and clear crystal quartz, tiger's eye, topaz

METAL: Gold

MESSAGES: Gold or orange ink on white paper

RULES: Abundance and prosperity where there has been a lack of it; all creative ventures, original ideas, and new beginnings; energy, joy, and health; buying and selling homes; problems relating to middle age; male and fathering issues; increasing self-confidence

GLOBALLY: Revival of barren land, overcoming drought, slowing down global warming

RESULTS: Within seven days

SIGNS OF FAVOUR: Being surrounded in golden sunbeams or seeing blue rays; finding a stray cat; hearing music unexpectedly near your home; seeing a golden butterfly

Anael or Hanael

ROLE: Archangel of love and marriage, usually associated with female energies

IMAGE: Surrounded by rose and green light, with silver wings, delicate features and hands full of roses

DAY: Friday

TIME OF DAY: Twilight

COLOURS: Green, pink

FRAGRANCES: Apple blossom, lemon verbena, rose, strawberry

TREES AND PLANTS: Coconut, all fruit trees, magnolia

FLOWERS AND HERBS: Delphinium, forget-me-not, lilac, lily and lily of the valley, valerian, vanilla, yarrow

CRYSTALS: Amethyst, emerald, jade, moss agate, pearl, pink or mangano calcite, rose quartz

METAL: Copper

MESSAGES: Green ink or white on pink paper

RULES: Beauty, love, marriage, the arts, music, the environment, families, reconciliation, and for gentle gradual growth or increase in all areas of life, from health and luck to money and business

GLOBALLY: Reforestation, preservation of mineral resources and earth's natural fuels

RESULTS: Within twenty-eight days

SIGNS OF FAVOUR: A late or early blooming rose; to see doves or blue birds; to be offered an apple(s); green mist or the smell of roses when none are present

Ariel

ROLE: Keeper of the sacred wisdom, guardian of prophecy, nature and healer of animals, birds, and fish

IMAGE: Mature with long silver hair and violet eyes, surrounded by yellow light, with a cloak of radiant white with rainbows at the hem

DAY: Friday

TIME OF DAY: Midafternoon

COLOUR: Violet

FRAGRANCES: Bergamot, cherry, any fruit fragrances

TREES AND PLANTS: Alder, manuka (New Zealand tea tree), moss

FLOWERS AND HERBS: Bluebell, lemon balm, lemon verbena, snowdrop

CRYSTALS: All earth jaspers and agates, such as Dalmatian jasper, leopardskin, moss and tree agate, snakeskin agate

METAL: Copper

MESSAGES: Dark green ink on white paper

RULES: Pet welfare and healing; relocation to the countryside or downsizing your home; finding a better-quality and maybe simpler way of life; environmental, animal, or people-focused careers; happy holidays and short breaks; developing psychic powers

GLOBALLY: Healing the ozone layer and mitigating over-intensive farming methods

RESULTS: Within six days or six weeks

SIGNS OF FAVOUR: Seeing an unusual number of young animals; a very early or late-budding flower; a plant you thought dead coming back to life; receiving a series of unrequested holiday brochures

Azrael

ROLE: A watcher or protector angel of the earth; guides souls after life to the heavens

IMAGE: Translucent with a halo that glows from within his whole body with black hooded cloak and wings

DAY: Tuesday

TIME OF DAY: Any

COLOUR: Dark or ruby red

CRYSTALS: Bloodstone, garnet, red aventurine, red tiger's eye, ruby

METAL: Stainless steel or tungsten

FRAGRANCES: Acacia, ginger, hibiscus, pine

TREES AND PLANTS: Cedar, cypress, firs and pines

FLOWERS AND HERBS: Basil, chrysanthemum, cyclamen, parsley, passion flower, saffron

RULES: Overcoming grief and sorrow, mastering obsessions or crippling fears, breaking free from a bully or a destructive situation, starting again, assisting necessary endings leading to beginnings

GLOBALLY: For protection against terrorism, germ warfare, and epidemics

RESULTS: Within seven days for urgent matters, more gradual for deeper sorrows

SIGNS OF FAVOUR: Discovering a strong-smelling new plant in your garden, being unexpectedly offered a spicy meal, seeing an unexpected cluster of bright red flowers growing, seeing an unusual memorial, or reading of an unconventional memorial service

Cassiel

ROLE: Archangel of stillness and compassion, great thinkers, and all ancient traditions, indigenous and developed

IMAGE: Bearded, riding a dragon, wearing dark robes with indigo flames sparking from his halo

DAY: Saturday

TIME OF DAY: Midnight (but any time after dark is fine)

COLOURS: Burgundy, dark purple, indigo, (also black, brown or grey)

FRAGRANCES: Ivy, mimosa, patchouli, sage, tea tree

TREES: Cypress, evergreens, yew

FLOWER AND HERBS: Carnation, celandine, coriander, pansy, rue, violet, wallflower

CRYSTALS: Fossils, hematite, jet, obsidian, onyx, black tourmaline, green aventurine, turitella agate, smoky quartz, snowflake obsidian

METALS: Lead or pewter

MESSAGES: Purple or black ink on white paper

RULES: Restoring balance, patience, all slow-moving matters, practical or financial worries, problems and opportunities concerning older or disabled people, living arrangements and any house renovations, healing or alleviating chronic illnesses and overwhelming sorrow or grief, inheritance, debt worries or problems with officialdom, also for the restoration of good luck

GLOBALLY: The conservation of ancient sites and beautiful buildings, the restoration of the knowledge and homelands of indigenous peoples

RESULTS: As long as three calendar months, but can be remarkably fast for an urgent need

SIGNS OF FAVOUR: To be given dried flowers, to hear from an elderly friend or relative unexpectedly, to find some fruit bitter or sour when you eat it, to find something made of lead or a dark-grey metal, seeing a picture of a tortoise or one in real life

Gabriel

ROLE: Archangel of the moon, carrying divine messages, regarded as having female energies

IMAGE: Clothed in silver or dark blue with a mantle of stars and a crescent moon for his halo, a golden horn and a white lily; alternatively, with a lantern in his right hand and a mirror of jasper in his left

DAY: Monday

TIME OF DAY: Sunset

COLOUR: Silver

FRAGRANCES: Jasmine, myrrh, rose

TREES: Eucalyptus, lemon, pear, weeping willow

FLOWERS AND HERBS: All small white flowers, iris, lotus, poppy, white rose

CRYSTALS: Moonstone, mother-of-pearl, opal, pearl, selenite

METAL: Silver

MESSAGES: Blue ink on white paper or silver ink on blue paper

RULES: Protection against inclement weather and natural disasters; for travel across water; for matters concerning women, infants, and children, mothering, pregnancy, childbirth, and fertility; for diminishing self-destructive tendencies; for peace in the home and at work; healing; psychic development and divination; keeping secrets

GLOBALLY: Protects water creatures, cleansing water, and protects against extreme seasonal effects

RESULTS: Within twenty-eight days

SIGNS OF FAVOUR: A dog barking outside your home, finding a silver coin or being given something silver, news of a birth or an unexpected invitation to a christening, a spider spinning its web in front of you, being surrounded by moonbeams or silver light

Jophiel, also called Iophiel and Zophiel

ROLE: Archangel of paradise and of joy

IMAGE: Yellow robes with an orange sunlike halo, radiating sunbeams, and with long blonde hair and pale yellow wings

COLOUR: Bright yellow

DAY: Sunday

TIME OF DAY: Around noon

FRAGRANCES: Grapefruit, lemongrass, lime, neroli

TREES AND PLANTS: Lemon, olive, orange, palms

FLOWERS AND HERBS: Chamomile, marigolds, rosemary, sunflower

CRYSTALS: Ametrine, citrine, golden topaz, honey calcite, rutilated quartz, smoky quartz, sunstone

METALS: Brass, bronze

MESSAGES: Gold on white

RULES: Learning new information, especially about spiritual matters, personal happiness, self-esteem, and self-love; overcoming food-related disorders; holidays or living in the sun; protection against bullies and emotional blackmail

GLOBALLY: Reducing scaremongering and manipulation by those who promote distrust

RESULTS: Within seven days

SIGNS OF FAVOUR: Dancing sunbeams on a dark day, seeing a mass of yellow flowers, meeting a number of people who are singing or whistling as they walk, an unusually warm or sunny day

Lumiel

ROLE: The light bringer, the morning star, and a major angel of teaching

IMAGE: Young with a white tunic, brilliant white cloak, and a blazing star on his brow

DAY: Sunday

TIME OF DAY: Noon, or when the sun is shining brightly

COLOUR: White

FRAGRANCES: Acacia, benzoin, linden blossom, sandalwood

TREES AND PLANTS: Tall strong trees like cedar, oak, redwood

FLOWERS AND HERBS: Angelica, hyssop, red and wild roses, Solomon's seal

CRYSTALS: Aqua and opal aura, amber, emerald, jet, meteorite, optical calcite

METAL: Platinum, white gold

MESSAGES: Dark brown ink on light blue paper

RULES: Any emergency and all matters concerning teaching and learning; contracts, stability of tenure, job security; original ideas and inventions; finding a new solution to an old problem

GLOBALLY: The preservation of the earth and her species

RESULTS: Within a week for urgent matters, six months for longer-term aims

SIGNS OF FAVOUR: Shafts of light on a dark day, seeing unusually bright stars, being given red roses or seeing them in unusual settings

Metatron

ROLE: Said to have once been mortal as the prophet Enoch; carries prayers between mortals and the heavens; the heavenly scribe. The guardian of all guardian angels

IMAGE: Tallest of the archangels, a pillar of light from which sparks flash, with thirty-six wings and eyes as brilliant as the sun; carries a pen and scroll, the contents of which are hidden

COLOURS: Maroon, white

DAY: Saturday

TIME OF DAY: Noon to 3 PM

FRAGRANCES: Frankincense, juniper, lemongrass, lime, myrrh, sandalwood

TREES AND PLANTS: Cedar, blackthorn, gorse, mistletoe, walnut, yew

FLOWERS AND HERBS: Carnation, clematis, orchid, parsley, sage, wisteria

CRYSTALS: Blue aventurine, flint, mahogany obsidian, sardonyx, tektite, titanium aura

METAL: Meteorite

MESSAGES: Purple ink on yellow paper or black ink on white paper

RULES: Any major life transformation or change, life reviews and changing life paths, all educational ventures, learning new skills (especially in later years), relocation abroad, protection against unfair criticism or inequality

GLOBALLY: For relieving child poverty and disease and protecting children who work in sweatshops in the Third World

RESULTS: Twelve months for slow-moving matters, a week for more urgent issues

SIGNS OF FAVOUR: An invitation to a local educational event, an unexpected letter or phone call from abroad, suddenly recalling or hearing the words of a poem you learned at school, news of an old school teacher or friend

Raphael

ROLE: The traveller's archangel and archangel of healing and the four winds

IMAGE: Carrying a golden vial of medicine and a traveller's staff, dressed in the colours of early morning sunlight, a green healing ray emanating from his halo

DAY: Wednesday

TIME OF DAY: Dawn

COLOURS: Green, grey, lemon-yellow

FRAGRANCES: Lavender, lemongrass, lemon balm

TREES AND PLANTS: Aspen, ferns, hazel, silver birch

FLOWERS AND HERBS: Daffodil, dill, fennel, lily of the valley, primrose

CRYSTALS: Ametrine, any agate, citrine, falcon's eye, lemon chrysoprase, malachite, onyx, serpentine, white sapphire, yellow jasper

METAL: Aluminium, platinum

MESSAGES: Black ink on yellow paper

RULES: Healing and health, business ventures, technological expertise, self-employment, short-distance travel and relocation, young people, successful buying and selling, protection against road or travel accidents, learning languages, writing, the media, tests and examinations, clear communication

GLOBALLY: For community matters, a free media everywhere and the dissemination of unbiased information

RESULTS: Within seven days, may be much faster

SIGNS OF FAVOUR: A bird flying into your house or against the window, a fern or weed springing up overnight, darting light beams, dreaming of monkeys or birds, unexpected visitors—one after the other

Raziel

ROLE: Archangel of divine mysteries and of secrets, credited with writing the esoteric *Book of the Angel Raziel*, which contained all earthly and heavenly knowledge

IMAGE: Swirling robes with deep green flares in his halo or as an outline behind a dark grey semi-transparent curtain

DAY: Saturday

TIME OF DAY: As it is getting dark or any misty day

COLOUR: Dark green

FRAGRANCES: Ambergris, any tree incenses, such as cedar, musk, myrrh

TREES AND PLANTS: Golden wattle, sycamore, any very old trees

FLOWERS AND HERBS: Fennel, lavender, musk, patchouli

CRYSTALS: any of the aura crystals such as cobalt, opal, aqua, or titanium aura, Apache tears, fossils, meteorite, opal, peridot, tektite

MESSAGES: Black on grey paper

RULES: All spiritual and psychic learning, especially astrology; for changing what seems an inevitable event or disaster; for keeping plans secret until you can carry them out

GLOBALLY: Religious and racial tolerance, the wise use of energy resources in the modern world

RESULTS: When least expected

SIGNS OF FAVOUR: The sun suddenly coming out through mist, a cobweb after rain covered in sunlight and jewelled raindrops, solving a minor mystery, being offered the loan of, or coming across, a book of sacred literature you bought years earlier

Sachiel

ROLE: The divine benefactor, archangel of charity and of good harvests

IMAGE: Deep blue and purple, carrying sheaves of corn with a rich purple and golden halo and blue and purple wings

DAY: Thursday

TIME OF DAY: Afternoon

COLOURS: Deep blue and purple

FRAGRANCES: Honeysuckle, sandalwood, sage, sagebrush

TREES AND PLANTS: Ash, beech, chestnut, Norwegian pine, oak

FLOWERS AND HERBS: Carnation, hyssop, iris, lotus, nutmeg, thyme, valerian

INCENSES: Honeysuckle, lotus, sage, sagebrush

CRYSTALS: Azurite, blue sapphire, blue topaz, chrysocolla, lapis lazuli, sodalite, turquoise

MESSAGES: Dark blue ink on white paper or blue ink on light purple paper

RULES: Justice, increasing abundance and prosperity, formal study, partnerships (both personal and in business), career advancement, leadership, long-distance travel and house moves, restoration after financial loss, redundancy, breakdowns, illness

GLOBALLY: For good harvests, for relieving lands where there is famine or disease, alleviating world poverty

RESULTS: Within seven days

SIGNS OF FAVOUR: Purple mist or dancing dusty light beams, a bee entering your home, finding acorns or a gold-coloured coin, dreaming of ships or journeys overseas, or you are unexpectedly offered purple grapes or flowers

Samael/Sammael

ROLE: Archangel of personal integrity, cleansing fire, and of overcoming all obstacles in the way of truth

IMAGE: In midnight blue and red, with blue and red flames in his halo and midnight blue wings, with a huge gleaming dark-gold sword

DAY: Tuesday

TIME OF DAY: Midnight (or late evening)

COLOURS: Indigo, red

FRAGRANCES: Acacia, cinnamon, cypress, dragon's blood, ginger, spices

TREES AND PLANTS: Fig, holly, rowan, monkey puzzle tree, thorns

FLOWERS AND HERBS: Asters, heather, hibiscus, mint, nettles, pine, tarragon, thyme

CRYSTALS: Blood or red agate, garnet, iron pyrites, red jasper, ruby, titanium aura

METALS: Iron, steel

MESSAGES: Red ink on white paper

RULES: Physical courage and strength; protection of the home, workplace, vehicles, and personal possessions; also guards against bullying, road rage, or accidents while commuting; malice, mind games, and psychic attack; male potency; independence; over-coming addictions, destructive habits, or bad influences; competitive sports; all in the armed forces or security services

GLOBALLY: Overcoming dictators, inhumane prisons, and terrorism; protecting those in war zones or former war zones

RESULTS: Within seven days

SIGNS OF FAVOUR: To dream of sheep, a sudden sense of warmth throughout your body, red light or mist, spilling pepper or another hot spice, finding a key, a candle suddenly flaring up or sparking

Uriel

ROLE: Angel of transformation and guardian of the earth and sun, who brought alchemy to humankind

IMAGE: Dressed in rich burnished gold and ruby red with a fiery sword, an open hand holding a flame, and a bright, flamelike halo blazing in the darkness; flashes of lightning

DAY: Tuesday or Saturday

TIME OF DAY: Midnight

COLOURS: Indigo, dark and ruby red

FRAGRANCES: Basil, copal (plant or tree resin), dragon's blood, ginger, sandalwood, tarragon

TREES AND PLANTS: Alder, any desert plants, cactus, laburnum

FLOWERS AND HERBS: Any large red flowers, parsley, pepper, poinsettia, tiger lily

CRYSTALS: Hematite, obsidian, rutilated quartz, tiger's eye

METAL: Brass, burnished gold

MESSAGES: Dark red ink on white

RULES: For protection of all kinds; overcoming anger or violence in others and transforming our own negative emotions into impetus for positive change; resolve when confronting a major ambition or obstacle; the power to fight on in dark times

GLOBALLY: To make the world a safer, better place

RESULTS: Within one month

SIGNS OF FAVOUR: Finding jewellery or some metal item you had lost; going to a new place with an open fire or fireplace; hearing of or seeing a chimney sweep; seeing an unusual number of fire engines in a day; seeing unexpected rainbows or a blue dragonfly

Zadkiel

ROLE: The most gentle archangel of healing and abundance, the performing arts, and all alternative therapies, but also brave in fighting injustice

IMAGE: Surrounded by pale blue light with sky-blue wings, with a ceremonial dagger and a white standard bearing the white background and red cross of Michael, whom he defends

DAY: Thursday

TIME OF DAY: Late morning

COLOUR: Sky blue

FRAGRANCES: Bergamot, magnolia, nutmeg, ylang ylang

TREES AND PLANTS: All gum trees, aspen, hazel, silver birch, white poplar

FLOWERS AND HERBS: Hyacinth, lily, rosemary, sweetgrass, tulip

CRYSTALS: Angelite, celestite, blue chalcedony, blue lace agate, blue or white howlite, blue quartz,

METAL: Tin, zinc

MESSAGES: Bright blue on white paper

RULES: Long-term prosperity; success in fulfilling personal dreams; overcoming fears, phobias, and anxiety; protecting against gossip, spite, and bad neighbours; for long or unexpected journeys; for receiving what is owed whether money, credit, or promotion; learning alternative therapies; all children's needs

GLOBALLY: Major charitable initiatives, especially to the Third World

RESULTS: Seven days

SIGNS OF FAVOUR: Finding or being given a beautiful stone or crystal, seeing a cloudless blue sky; receiving an unexpected bonus or rebate

Writing archangel letters, e-mails, or texts

In the ancient world, letters to the archangels were one of the most common ways of asking for their protection and inspiration, and were written in one of the old angelic scripts.

I would recommend writing an initial letter to the archangels as a way of calling in that extra power and determination to help yourself, as well as attracting good fortune or protection if you feel vulnerable. However, since this is a book for busy people, having written your initial letter, you can then go high-tech and send archangel e-mails or even send an angelic text message on your mobile phone.

Ideally, work with someone who accepts the power of the angels to assist (and you would do the same for them). In this case, you would send regular updates and messages to the archangel that your friend would pick up on his or her phone or computer. They would then, as soon as possible and with eyes closed, focus on your message, allowing an answer to come to them that would be sent back to you. Alternatively, you could send empowering angelic messages to a cheap pay-as-you-go phone of your own kept for this purpose, or to another unused e-mail account of yours. Then, when you have time, focus on what you mailed to the archangel and an answer or unexpected words in your mind or signs in daily life may follow.

CREATING MORE FORMAL ARCHANGEL LETTERS

+ Decide which archangel can best help with your needs (if in doubt, pass a pendulum over the list of archangels on pages 192–205). If possible, choose the day of the archangel and his or her special time and sit in your angel place with the right coloured ink and paper.

+ Light your archangel candle and fragrance incense stick from the central candle.

+ Drop a single pinch of salt into the flame of the archangel candle and ask for protection or inspiration in the days ahead. You may sense the archangel's presence, and the fragrance may become intense.

+ Try to write the letter spontaneously so it contains pure undiluted feelings. Emotions are a powerful channel of connection with the psychic world.

+ Begin with a greeting such as *Beloved, Dear, or Wise Archangel* (name him or her). Let the words flow about the matter you are seeking help, using as many or as few words as you wish. You do not need to use elevated words like *thee* or *thou*.

+ If you are writing about a personal concern, then perhaps incorporate a more global aspect as well, if relevant. You have every right to ask for what you need and you may be given a little more.

+ End the letter with whatever feels right, with thanks or in hope, and sign your first name or your special angel name as described in chapter 2 (see page 30).

+ Put the letter in a blank envelope and seal it with a few drops of wax from the candle (or sealing wax).

+ Blow out the candle but leave the incense to burn. Finish by naming the archangel three times, saying, *"Blessings be on all."*

+ When the wax is dry, put the letter in a box with a lid or in a plain folder in your angel place.

+ You can reread the letter on the angel's own day.

As I suggested, you can use e-mails or text messages to update the situation or to ask the archangel questions, but for some people, just writing the letter is enough.

Archangels are there to help. If you can do something small for the archangel's global causes or offer kindness to someone in need, you will feel you are saying "thank you" in a practical way.

ten

ANGEL BLESSINGS THROUGHOUT LIFE AND BEYOND

At birth and death as well as during our lives on Earth, angels are with us. It is said that Gabriel seals the lips of every child before birth so he or she will not reveal the secrets of heaven, and for this reason we all have a cleft above our mouth. It is also believed that the infant's spirit enters through the fontanelle, the crown of the head where the three skull bones fuse, which closes soon after birth and that the angels in the heavens cry a little as this is sealed. The fontanelle is the highest energy centre of the human body and the chakra that connects us with the higher realms of spirit.

Azrael, the mighty archangel I described in the last chapter, is also believed to guard every new infant on its journey from the womb and, when life ends, to guide the departing soul to the heavens wrapped in his warm cloak as the spirit rises again as light. It is said this gigantic angel notes every leaf that falls.

A NEAR-DEATH ANGELIC EXPERIENCE

The most tangible proof of angels carrying us to the afterlife is offered by near-death experiences, in which a person momentarily dies during an operation or heart attack or due to an accident, for example. Such experiences have been collected even from children by researchers and doctors, and are remarkably consistent.

Joan, who lives in New Zealand, describes her encounter:

Ten years ago I had an aortic aneurysm and, according to the doctors, it was a near miracle I survived. At some point, either during the operation or while I was in intensive care afterwards, I floated upwards into a beautiful blue sky and met with beings made of mist who spoke to me telepathically. The misty beings were of human shape and surrounded by the kind of clear blue sky you see on a beautiful summer's day. At first, it looked as if the beings were wearing cornettes (the wide hats nuns used to wear) but they could have been folded wings behind their bodies. There were three at first, but one disappeared as if going behind an invisible curtain, and the remaining two came towards me. I felt very light, and free of my body. I was aware I had left my family behind, but I knew they would be okay. The angelic telepathic message was clear: *You have to go back.* I felt very disappointed, but turned and found myself at some point later in a hospital bed on the road to recovery.

My surgeon said afterwards that it was a miracle I had survived a ruptured aneurysm, as he had never been able to save previous casualties in all the years he had been practising.

Coming Forth to Carry Me Home

I have over the previous twenty years collected numerous experiences of dying people who have seen angels shortly before death. Even if relatives have not witnessed the angel, they frequently report the sick person momentarily looks like their former healthy self and may be able to talk clearly even if previously semiconscious or unconscious.

+ Jane from north London described how, when she worked in hospitals, she would see orbs of light become an angelic form by a bed if someone was close to passing over.

+ Anne from the north of England was visiting her father in a nursing home. One afternoon he spoke about a beautiful woman calling him from outside the window (on the first floor with no balcony). The next day he said clearly and coherently that his angel was waiting outside the window for him. He died shortly afterwards, smiling.

+ Margaret, who lives in Cork, Ireland, was seventeen when she heard a choir singing outside the front of her house at about 11 PM. Her mother seemed unaware of the sound, and so Margaret said nothing. The following morning, Margaret's aunt Katherine told Margaret's mother that *her* daughter Kathleen had heard a choir at the back of their house (some distance away) at around 11 PM. Aunt Katherine had heard nothing. The families later discovered that the girls' great-aunt had died at a hospital, miles away, at 11 PM.

+ Jane, a nurse near London, was caring for Nicholas, a seven-year-old boy dying from cystic fibrosis (this was twenty years ago, when little could be done). He was being cuddled on his mother's lap when he opened his eyes and said: "Mummy, I can see the angels." Soon afterwards he died.

+ Pauline was sitting by her dying mother. Her mother, who had been semiconscious for days, became suddenly alert, smiled, and told Pauline that she could see a beautiful angel. Seeing

Pauline's shocked expression, she laughed and, with her customary humour not heard since the illness had become acute, joked, "Now you really *do* think I am batty." Then she lapsed into unconsciousness, but looked totally at peace. Pauline was aware of a light surrounding her mother. Her mother was pronounced dead soon afterwards and the light disappeared. Hospital staff were adamant that her mother could not have regained full consciousness, and so Pauline said nothing more.

♦ When Nancy's mother died, Nancy saw at the funeral not an angel, but her mother's spirit in the form of white rays. She explained, "I was thirty-eight when my mother died. While the coffin stood in the church, I definitely saw my mother's spirit rise and leave her body as a substance made up of white rays the same size as her body, though without form. The white rays drifted to the side of the coffin and then upwards till they were three or four feet over the coffin and then disappeared. No one else shared my experience."

Angels and Bereavement

Angels can also comfort us when we are grieving for a deceased relative or cannot reach the stage of grieving openly. Debbie's mother-in-law died after being knocked over by a motorist and the family was badly traumatised. Debbie, who lives in South Africa, says each member of the family retreated into their own bubbles of private sorrow.

One evening, Debbie was in the shower and the bathroom was filled with an amazing yellow and white light. An angel appeared in front of her. He said, *"Why are you worrying so much? Give the angels your problems and we will help you."* The water in the shower kept running, but above her head no water was falling on her face or body while the angel was talking to her. Once the angel spoke to her, she immediately felt a calming and loving feeling come over her, and

Debbie was able to help the family to come together to grieve. She was able from the appearance of the angel to identify him as Jophiel, archangel of joy.

Angels can in times of bereavement give us signs that the loved one is still with us when we are blocked by grief. When a loved one dies and grief is still new and raw, particular items they wanted us to have can seem the only link with the deceased person.

When Jayne's mother died, the rings she had bequeathed to Jayne in her will were missing. Since these included her mother's wedding ring, Jayne was heartbroken, and asked the angels to help her find them.

Weeks later, as Jayne was clearing her mother's house, she could feel her mother's presence, as if she was sitting in her favourite chair. Jayne heard her mother's voice say, "I knew it would be you doing the clearing up. I am so pleased." Jayne cried and desperately wanted her mother to hug her. As she dusted the sideboard, a tiny white feather floated down from the ceiling and landed in front of her hand. Jayne knew at that moment that the angels were also with her.

Jayne was packing up to go home when she felt a gentle push- ing sensation in the middle of her back, and was guided towards the kitchen at the back of the house. Jayne's sister had promised to clean the kitchen, and so Jayne was cross to see the chaos. Jayne was still holding her feather when she felt another gentle push in the middle of her back and, this time, was guided to a corner cupboard. Auto- matically, Jayne began to take the very dusty china and glasses out of the cupboard. After throwing away most of the crockery, she was about to shut the cabinet door when she saw an old egg cup hidden at the back of a shelf. In it were her mother's missing rings. Jayne is convinced that the angels had helped her mother show her where the precious rings were.

Drawing comfort from the angels

When someone close dies, we miss their physical presence, and it may seem trite to ask your angels to help you. If you were not able to say goodbye or there were unresolved emotional issues between you, bereavement may seem doubly hard.

Of course, even angelic help will not take away the pain, but especially if you are alone, you can ask for the support of the angels in the difficult days and months ahead. For Debbie it was Jophiel who came, but other bereaved people sense the presence of Iris with her rainbow wings or Carina, the motherly angel who wraps us in her blue cloak and rocks us if we cry in the night. It might even be Azrael who, if he cares about a leaf falling, will certainly assist you in sorrow. You will find details in the Angel Treasury in chapter 12 (see page 227) and previous chapters of this and other comforting angel books.

The following are suggestions for ways of using angelic help:

+ Make your angel place or angel healing table a focus for remembering and celebrating the life of the person you have lost. Put their photograph and a memento there, such as a piece of their jewellery or a scarf.

+ Add a bunch of their favourite flowers or a potted plant. For me, it is always hyacinths for my late mother; she planted hyacinth bulbs to bring spring to our inner city backyard.

+ Place a little of the person's favourite fragrance in a small dish or, for an elderly male relative, maybe a bowl of their favourite pipe tobacco.

+ Light a white candle after dark and, inhaling the fragrance or holding the memento, speak aloud all the things you wanted to say and maybe did not get a chance. Ask the angels to carry the words to your relative in the afterlife, or however that place seems to you.

+ Even if you believe death is the end, try this anyway and you may receive reassuring signs.

✦ You may feel the presence of an angel or sense your deceased relative, lover, or friend touching your hair or brow gently. You need fear nothing for you are surrounded only by love and angelic protection.

✦ Blow out the candle and send love to your lost one.

✦ If you have children, allow them to light a candle each in the heart of the home. Get out your favourite family photos and ask the angels to send love to their great-grandma or granddad.

✦ Use this family time to share happy memories, family jokes, and pictures of the family together or of Great-Grandma when she was young and very serious at her wedding.

✦ In the daytime, go not to the cemetery but to places where you and the deceased person were once happy together, whether this is a tea shop or a beach or park where you used to walk together.

✦ Ask the guardian angels of the place to restore happy memories and to bring you both close for a moment across the dimensions. Buy or take home something small from the place and, if outdoors, leave a small angel crystal in return (see pages 35–36).

✦ On birthdays and special anniversaries of the loved one's life (not just the anniversary of the death), cook their favourite family recipes and if you have children, make a small cake for granny in heaven. Even if you are smiling through your tears ask the angels to bless the occasion; you could also re-run those awful home movies. You may become aware of soft laughter and a sense of the love that has never left you but was masked by grief.

✦ If you cannot make the connection, before bedtime light a white candle and put the fragrance near your bed or add a drop to your pillow. Ask Muriel or one of the other angels of sleep (see pages 60–61) to bring your loved one to you in a dream. Say a few words to the loved one, blow out the candle and, as you drift into sleep, picture their face smiling. Even if you do not dream of them that night, you may in the days ahead receive a sign, such as hearing their favourite tune on the radio or seeing their favourite flower in an unusual place.

eleven

MESSAGES FROM THE ANGELS

Angels have inspired and helped people from all walks of life throughout history. In this chapter, many of these well-known angels' characteristics and messages have been summarised, along with those of lesser-known angels who are especially helpful in offering guidance in the modern world.

THE ANGEL JOE SUNSHINE

The Reverend Shé d'Montford from the Gold Coast of Australia was desperate because her violent ex-husband had abducted their young son. The police were unable to help and she had spent all her money on private investigators, to no avail.

Walking down the street one day in total despair, her attention was drawn by a dazzling light from a crystal suspended in the window of a bookstore. It got brighter, disorientating her, and as Shé moved away she collided with a lamppost. Angry, she entered the store to complain, but a man near a bookshelf diverted her attention. He was tall with white-blonde hair and wore a yellow t-shirt and white jeans. The stranger took a book from the shelf and handed it to her.

"You should read this," he told her. *"If angels went through what you have been through, they would split and fall."*

On his shirt were the words "martial arts" and a phone number from another area. Shé needed to learn to defend herself as her ex-husband was a bully. The man gave her the phone number of a friend who taught martial arts locally. The stranger said his own name was Joe, but people called him "Sunshine."

Shé looked at the book and on the cover was a woman remarkably like herself and a beautiful male who resembled Joe, but with angel wings. Shé looked up, but Joe was gone.

Shé went to the counter with the book and told the assistant the man by the bookshelf had recommended it. The assistant looked surprised, and said there had been no customers in the store for over an hour. Shé paid and left hurriedly, hoping to catch up with Joe Sunshine, but he was not there. However, that chance meeting instantly put her life back on course. She rang the local martial arts expert, who incidentally had never heard of anybody called Joe or Sunshine who took martial arts lessons. The next time she faced her abusive ex-husband, he was unable to victimise her. She grew stronger emotionally and eventually, through her new strength and determination, regained custody of her son. What's more, Shé was inspired to open a spiritual retreat and has become an author, television personality, and editor of an esoteric magazine. Shé later found out that the angel of sunshine and happiness is Jophiel, and his colour is yellow.

So, even an archangel can appear in twenty first-century garb and is just as likely to wear a yellow t-shirt as golden robes.

Using the 250-Angel Oracle

The angel list in the final chapter (see page 227) may be a useful resource if you want to find out more about a specific angel name; for that reason I have listed them alphabetically. If the same name regularly appears to you, there may be some aspect of your life linked with that angel to which you need to pay attention. But first, I will suggest how you can use divination to indicate the name of the angel whose knowledge and wisdom you need to answer a question.

✿ FIND YOUR ANGEL FOR THE DAY AHEAD

Select at random the name of one angel from the list in the final chapter to guide you in the day ahead. The message of this angel will suggest the actions or prevailing energies most likely to bring success during the day. You do not have to choose an angel every day unless you wish to.

+ Early in the morning or last thing at night before bed, ask your guardian angel to guide your hand when you pass your crystal pendulum a few centimetres above each name. Move your hand slowly until you feel your pendulum or hand vibrating and pulling down over one name (see pages 38–42 to remind yourself about using a pendulum). That will be the angel who will be most helpful.

+ Even if the angelic purpose is not immediately obvious, repeat the angel's name during the day in your mind and an image may come of the angel and of the way the angel can help. Sometimes the angels can indicate a situation that will come to pass within twenty-four hours, or a strength you will need during that twenty-four-hour period.

✿ USING THE 250 NAMES TO ANSWER A QUESTION

Choose up to three angels from the list to answer a specific question. The combined messages of the three angels will provide an answer.

+ First, light a white candle and floral incense, then name aloud your question and ask for the guidance of your guardian angel in selecting the three angels.

+ Pass your pendulum slowly over each name until you have selected three angels. Write the names and messages on separate pieces of white paper in green ink.

+ Close your eyes and allow any insights or images to come into your mind about the three angels, but do not force connections.

+ Now under each message in turn allow your hand to carry on writing. Your words may explain the connections between the three messages and possible courses of action or resolution.

+ You may feel the hand you write with vibrate slightly and have the feeling that someone is guiding it. This does not mean that you are being taken over by an angel—rather that your hand is transmitting a message via your higher personal angelic connection. You can stop at any time.

+ When you sense your hand slowing, read what you have written. It may be poetry, part of a song, or information that will answer the question or issue that has concerned you, or which will offer guidance to a future step.

Making your own angel cards

You may find you are drawn to certain angels on the list, or you may pick recurring daily angels that relate closely to your life. Note these names down and once you have built up a core set of between twenty-five and fifty angel names, you can create a card pack to use to select your angel of the day and to answer questions. Unlike commercial packs, these are unique to you and doubly powerful.

- For a basic set, use white or pastel-coloured cards (stick to one colour) about the size of a playing card, one for each angel you have selected.

- Write the name of the angel on one side with a few words to summarise his or her energies; for example, for Jophiel *sunshine and joy*.

- Then laminate or cover both sides of the card with clear tape to keep them clean.

- You can illustrate the cards if you wish. You could use angelic images from the Internet (allowed on certain sites for noncommercial purposes). Choose ones that portray each angel as best as possible.

Using your own card oracle

- To discover your angel of the day, shuffle the pack with blank sides up. Place the cards in a fan shape, face down on the table, and use the palm of your hand or your pendulum to select one. Alternatively, pick one at random from the pack.

Simple angel card layouts to ask questions

- Shuffle the pack and divide it into three approximately equal piles, face down.

+ Name your question and pick a card from the first pack to give you the angel who will reveal what you need to leave behind or change.

+ Pick a card from the second pack to represent the action you need to take now, or helpful factors that will move the matter forward.

+ Finally, select a card from the third pack to indicate the possible outcome of the suggested action or influence in pack 2. The selected cards should be placed side by side and read left to right in order of selection.

+ If the matter is not clear, pick a resolution card from any of the three packs, which will bring the messages together.

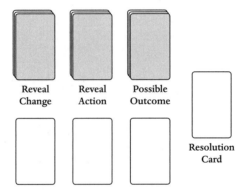

+ Alternatively, if you have a choice to make between two options, divide the cards after shuffling into two approximately equal piles and select three from each pile to give you the steps you would take for each of the two options.

+ Make a column of the three cards for each option.

+ If the best option is not clear, add a fourth card to each row to represent the likely outcome.

+ You can add a final card at the top and between the two columns for a final verdict.

+ You can use any of these methods to answer questions for friends or family. Allow them to shuffle and choose the cards.

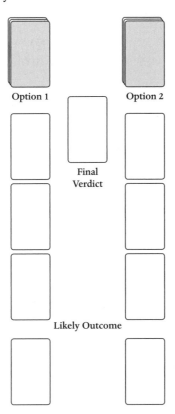

Eleanor's angel question

Eleanor had ended a long-term relationship because Tom, her partner, did not want marriage or children. She had been wondering whether to give up her well-paid but boring job in a bank, which has enabled her to travel, to train as a teacher of special needs. This would involve living with her parents and, in spite of grants, giving up her international lifestyle.

In Column 1 that she decided was "leave banking," she picked the following cards:

Bardiel, the angel of hail and temporary disruption. He warned her decision to give up her lifestyle would not be easy, but would ultimately lead to her personal growth.

Nanael, the angel of learning, especially relating to disabilities. Eleanor had a disabled sister who had died, so she knew the reality of what she was training for.

Anael, archangel of love, marriage, and children. This was unexpected, but Eleanor knew if she stayed in banking she might well end up staying with Tom and giving up any hope of a family of her own.

In Column 2 was the option of staying as she was:

Anual, angel of financial stability. Eleanor loved the travel, but in her heart she was more and more aware of how shallow her life had become.

Alphun, angel of forgiveness and compromise. Part of her wanted to go back to Tom, whom she loved, but she knew he would never change his mind about children or family life.

Bahram, angel of victory, advised Eleanor to carry on, even though life in banking seemed unsatisfactory. She knew that she could go far in banking, but it was not what she wanted.

Eleanor picked a final card. It was **Afriel,** protector of the young or vulnerable, who said that even if she was scared, she should go ahead bravely.

I never saw Eleanor again, but I heard through a friend that she was working in a unit for autistic children and was pregnant by her new partner, another teacher at the school.

Angels Everywhere

Even if you study angels for thirty years and read every book on the market on angel wisdom, you are not guaranteed a full-blown golden angel visitation. Nevertheless, even in the first weeks of talking to your angels, increasingly you will become aware of angelic presences, support, protection, and inspiration in every aspect of your life. However, you will not find your overdraft miraculously wiped out or discover that your great-aunt, whom you have consistently failed to please since you were eighteen months old, turns into Mary Poppins overnight!

Sometimes, too, you have to look for signs of angelic help—not from the skies, but in an unexpected kindness from a fellow human who maybe can ill afford the time or resources, but does so willingly. For angel energies do not exist solely "out there," but are powers for good that can bring out the best in others and in ourselves.

As I said in the Introduction, Emanuel Swedenborg believed we all have the power to become angels. So rather than waiting for the ideal moment or a flurry of white feathers to bring you the winning lottery ticket or the guy or gal of your dreams, spread your own wings to make your dreams come true. Smile even at unfriendly people and spread positive vibes, even when you feel like crawling into a hole. Take five minutes watching the sunset out of the office window instead of the computer screen and feel the angel magic that is yours, everywhere, because it is within you.

twelve

THE ANGEL TREASURY

A Treasury of 250 Angels

Abarthur, angel of the Pole Star, is dressed in star-studded robes; he turns the world on its axis. Aim for what you want, for you have the necessary foundations for success.

Abdiel, the fiery red and gold seraph, is as tall as a hundred men. Do not let anyone bully you or talk down to you.

Achaiah, the angel who knows the secrets of nature, wears autumnal colours. Even in the centre of a city or an unpromising situation, look for beauty and possibilities.

Adnachiel, the angel of learning and exploration, wears bright yellow robes. Learn something new, as this will lead to new people and places.

Adriel, the misty, silvery angel of the first week of the waning moon, helps with love under difficulty and says if you persevere in any relationship issue, it may be resolved.

Afriel, surrounded in green and blue mists, with a silver sword to drive away all harm from the young or nursing animal mothers. Even if you are scared, go forward bravely, for you will be protected.

Aftiel, angel of twilight, has wings and robes of misty grey. Send a blessing to someone who has angered you to free you from carrying the pain.

Akatriel, an angel with gold wings, robe, and halo. He is the golden angel of prayer. Be sure that what you pray or ask for is what you really want.

Aladiel, the angel who calms excess emotions, has silvery blue wings. Do not be emotionally pressured by a drama king or queen.

Alphun, the angel of doves and forgiveness, has soft feathery wings. It is time to compromise, for you may not get what you want on this occasion.

Ambriel, the angel of travel, wears the colours of early morning sunlight. Look further away, whether in cyberspace or reality, for what you need.

Amnixiel, angel of the last day of the waning moon, has a single star in her halo. Let go of worry and of what did not work out.

Amutiel, angel of the week after the full moon, has pure white robes and a pale, shimmering blue halo. To accept necessary changes, you must first let go of fear.

Anael, Aniel, or **Haniel,** the archangel of love and fidelity, is surrounded by roses. Love yourself as you are and for what you are, and not some impossible ideal.

Anafiel is a tall angel of pure light. Uncertainty will end and unexpected support or approval will come.

Anahita, a female angel in brown robes, protects the planet. Routine and obligations may temporarily delay more exciting plans.

Anauel, the angel of financial stability, has copper wings and a coppery golden halo. A drain on your resources will lessen.

Anpiel, angel of all birds, wears his cloak of a thousand feathers. There is now a chance to spread your wings and show a different side of yourself.

Ardousta, the female angel of generosity, has robes that flow like water. Allow others to give back to you and, above all, be generous to yourself.

Ariel, the archangel of nature, has rainbow robes. Do not lose sight of for whom and what you are working.

Armait, the golden-haired angel, brings truth and kindness into the world. Remember that you cannot be all things to all people.

Aruru, the angel who helped create humans from the soil of the earth, has golden brown wings and a halo like sun-touched grain crops. It may be possible to rebuild a crumbling relationship or situation.

Asaliah, the fiery angel, puts right injustice. You will get justice once you let go of the understandable desire for revenge.

Asariel, the archangel of the waves, carries a golden trident. Put into motion the first steps of a long-term travel or relocation plan.

Ashmodel or **Asmodel** is an angel of beauty, with soft pink rays. Value your beauty and ignore those who try to make you feel bad.

Asrael or **Azrael,** the archangel of fire, is translucent and glowing with a black hooded coat and black wings. He sees the smallest leaf fall. If something or someone is making you unhappy, deal with it, however trivial.

Assiel, angel of healing waters and crystals, has healing light radiating from his hands. Do not worry about your health or that of a loved one.

Atheniel, angel of the old moon, has a single star in her grey hair. Do not waste time regretting what or who never was: happiness is far closer to home than you realise.

Atliel is angel of the full moon, shimmering silver and gold. Act now and you will soon attract fertility in the way you most need it.

Attarib, ruling angel of the winter, has shimmering frost wings. The world will still turn if you slow down a bit. Step back from stress.

Azariel, angel of the new crescent moon, is surrounded by soft light. Wish hard enough for what you most want, and it will come true.

Azkariel, with silver trumpet and scroll, is the angel of proclamations. Long-awaited good news of family joy and celebration arrives.

Bahram, angel of victory, holds a banner of red and gold. Do not give up, as the desired end is almost in sight.

Barbelo is a beautiful golden female angel of gifts. Look for an opportunity to develop a hidden talent that you had put aside as impractical.

Bardiel, angel of hail, wears robes of sparkling white. A desired new beginning brings temporary disruption but long-term happiness.

Bariel, angel of small miracles, wears the colours of sunset. Unexpected help will come, but avoid repeating past mistakes.

Barkiel or **Barakiel** is archangel of lightning and good luck. Seize an unexpected opportunity and take a chance.

Baruch is guardian angel of the Tree of Life, brandishing a golden sword. Do not allow past mistakes or failures stop you from trying again.

Bath Kol, the heavenly voice, calls out in the darkness to all who are afraid. Unspoken fears about a loved one will not materialise.

Behemiel, angel of farms and helper of animals, has rich brown wings. Be patient and show extra tolerance in a coming slow period.

Beniel, angel of invisibility, is almost transparent. Keep a low profile and avoid interruptions and intrusions just now.

Bethor, supreme angel, has 29 thousand angels to serve him. Make quiet time at home to restore your inner harmony.

Boel, the purple-clad angel, holds the keys to the four corners of the world. Present restrictions and delays will lessen.

Cabet is the angel in blue robes who brings good crops and abundance. Success will result from money-spinning ideas or creative ventures.

Caila, angel of the Word of God, flies through heaven with eagle-winged sandals. Your ideas and viewpoint will be accepted by those who once refused to listen.

Caliel is the angel who protects all in dangerous places with his huge silver sword. You are spending valuable energy worrying, so either act or let go of fear.

Cambiel is called the watcher or guardian archangel. Wait for the right moment rather than leap in feet first now.

Caphriel is the angel who breaks down barriers as he strides across the earth. Though now may not be an ideal time for action, press ahead anyway.

Carina, the blue angel with a wool cloak, rocks the sorrowing in her arms. Talk to an understanding person or expert rather than lie awake worrying.

Cassiel, the gentle archangel, weeps for the sorrows of the world. A hurt will pass, but be gentle with yourself.

Catharel, angel of gardens and gardeners, emanates green rays. If you persist, this will be time for gradual growth or improvement in your life.

Causub is the angel who protects against snakes and human spite. Ignore gossip and rumours, and verify what people tell you.

Cerviel is the strong, tall angel who assisted David in defeating the giant Goliath. You will overcome a seemingly overwhelming situation if you fight back.

Chairoum, angel of the north, has snow-white wings. Do not give up on someone close who is being difficult.

Chamuel or **Camael,** archangel of courage, rides a leopard. Be brave. A petty bully will back down if tackled.

Charity is a gentle, white-robed angel, who carries food to nourish the hungry. Daughter of Sophia, she is an angel of wisdom. Give someone the benefit of the doubt, as you may have been too hasty.

Chavaquiah is the angel of silence, whose presence is felt, not seen. For now, say nothing—even if you are being pressured for an opinion or decision.

Chur, angel of the sun moving across the skies, drives a chariot of gold. Make sure you get credit for your input and ideas.

Cochabiel radiates bright starlight, and is starry angel of the planets, asteroids, and Milky Way. Discarded or unfulfilled dreams can still come true in a different way.

Dalquiel is the angel of illumination, whose halo flickers with golden flames. A long-standing problem can be solved by investigating a previously unavailable option.

Damabiah, angel of safe travel, has a map of the universe. Double-check any travel arrangements or entertainment tickets to avoid last-minute hitches.

Daniel, angel of official matters, carries a pen and scroll. It is time to sort out paperwork and pay attention to necessary details.

Derdekea, a female angel who lives on Earth, protects homes. It's time to tackle a domestic matter or chore you've been avoiding.

Dirachiel is a shimmering, early waxing moon angel. Secrets that burden you will soon be lifted and the welcome truth comes into the open.

Donquel, angel of true love and passion, has scarlet sparkling wings. Any love matter is favoured. Unspoken but desired words may be heard at last.

Duma is the silvery female angel of quiet sleep. Go to bed earlier for a night or two and avoid working right up until bedtime.

Elaiah, angel of starlight, is surrounded by silver beams. Avoid illusions and pretending someone or something is what it is not. Enjoy the reality.

Elemiah is the red and gold angel of commuters and all who drive for a living. Visit a place you like to go to occasionally to restore enthusiasm and spontaneity.

Eloa, female angel of compassion, was born from a tear shed by Jesus. Someone who is being a pain is acting out of unhappiness. Can you help?

Enediel is misty angel of the hidden moon. An unclear situation will resolve itself within two or three days.

Ergediel is the golden angel of the day before the full moon. It is time for a personal power infusion and focusing on boosting your energy levels and happiness.

Exael, angel of perfume, precious metals, and gems, has jewel-studded wings. Emotional fulfilment is as vital as material resources.

Faith, the second gentle daughter of Sophia, is an angel of wisdom. Have faith if your question is "What's the point of it all?"

Gabamiah, angel of song, plays a long golden horn. Step away from the noisy modern world and seek moments of solitude.

Gabriel, archangel of the moon, fertility, and the happy home, has a silver crescent halo. Make small, long-overdue changes so your home becomes a sanctuary from the world.

Gadriel, the purple-robed angel, works against wars between nations and religions. Try to reconcile disputes around you without taking sides.

Galgaliel, angel of sunshine, scatters sunbeams. Whatever is blocking your energies from the next (overdue) stage in love or life will clear.

Gavreel is the angel of peaceful solutions. You may need to work or live alongside difficult people for a time, so minimise touchiness and conflict.

Gazardiel is the angel who rules over the rising and setting sun. Leave behind at sunset what did not work out, be ready for the new beginning at dawn.

Gediel, angel of high places, has silver-pointed wings. Look upwards and over the horizon to the future rather than focusing on what is slowing you down.

Geliel shimmers through mist, with silver and gold wings and halo. He is an angel of the late waning moon. It may be possible to mend a relationship, even if the other person is being stubborn.

Gurid is a midsummer angel whose halo is made of all summer flowers. Make time for fun and don't take yourself or life too seriously.

Haaiah or **Haaimiah** is angel of peace and diplomacy, who wears silky grey robes. A future family or social gathering will be unexpectedly harmonious.

Habuiah, angel of abundance and fertility, has a halo like the noonday sun. Good fortune is coming and finances will soon be on the upturn.

Hadraniel has rich green wings and halo. He is the angel of lasting love throughout life, in sickness and health, hard times and good. Rely on loyalty to weather any difficult relationship or friendship.

Hael is an angel of beauty and art. Try a new look that pleases you, and others will be impressed.

Hahael with a rainbow halo, cares for aid and charity workers. You may need to show kindness to someone you do not like, but it will be repaid.

Hahaziah, the angel of spiritual awareness, has a pale-blue halo and halo. Make time to meditate, even for five minutes, as this will inspire your busy world.

Hahueuiah or **Hahaiah** is the angel of tradition, with indigo halo and wings. Stick to your principles, but let restrictive prohibitions based in childhood go.

Hakamiah, the angel who guards against treachery, holds a huge golden shield. In times of temptation, rely on old friends rather than new acquaintances, however exciting.

Hamaiel or **Hamaliel,** angel of perfection, is surrounded by misty forest green. Clear away unnecessary clutter, actual or emotional, in your life.

Hamayrod, angel of the time before sleep, has feathery blue wings. End each day at peace and do not let the sun go down on anger.

Hamied is the dazzling white angel of miracles. Even if other avenues have so far failed, help is at hand.

Harahel is the silver-grey angel of books and writing. You will soon receive a letter or e-mail that will bring news you hoped for.

Hariel is the golden-brown angel of pets and horses. Spend time with your pet or watching wildlife, and your perspective and good humour will return.

Haurvatat, female angel of wholeness, carries a full moon sphere. This is a day when you will be very powerful. Do not let temporary restlessness distract you from your goal.

Hayyel, angel caretaker of wild animals and endangered species, has green robes and carries a horn. Trust your instincts rather than listen to others.

Haziel is the angel who brings light into the darkness. What seems depressing right now will be more hopeful within twenty-four hours.

Helemeth is a pure white angel of radiant light. Believe in yourself more and do not be overly modest about your abilities.

Hochmel, angel of wisdom, carries a book containing all knowledge. What you need to know will come in your dreams or as a sign in your everyday world.

Hope, the third daughter of Sophia, wears white with sunshine-yellow wings and halo. Be optimistic and put a positive spin on events, for all will turn out well after all.

Hormuz, the green-winged angel, rules over the first day of each month. Make a plan for the year ahead and try to achieve at least one of your aims before the month ends.

Humiel is the practical angel who helps us with DIY. The right assistance will come along to resolve a practical domestic problem if you ask people you know.

Iahhel, angel of light, offers his hand to anyone who is lost or alone. Being alone is not the same as being lonely, which you can be if you are in the wrong company.

Iameth is the angel who calms tempestuous seas with his golden staff. Unexpected positive intervention will get someone off your back.

Iehalel, wise angel of justice, defends all unfairly accused or treated. Some new input or person will help to bring closure to any injustices or unresolved disputes.

Ieilael is the angel of the future we have yet to make. Beware of unnecessary financial commitments, as this puts restrictions on future plans.

Ihiazel is the angel of negotiations, with soft grey robes. A work or neighbourhood dispute may be resolved by someone unexpectedly moving on.

Imamiah is the angel of long-distance travel and protector against terrorism. Minimise risks involving any form of travel, then trust you will be protected by your angels.

Iris, angel of the rainbow, casts tiny rainbows as she flies. Quarrels can be mended, but do not blame yourself for what was not your fault.

Isda, a motherly angel of nourishment, carries a basket of bread. Care for your health, eat and exercise regularly, but do not set yourself impossible standards.

Israfel is another angel of song and choral music. Everyday rush is blocking important messages from your wise inner voice and angels. Take time out to listen.

Jamaerah, the wish angel, is surrounded by rainbow bubbles. Find the means to fulfil your own dreams, rather than wait for others or for good fortune.

Jazariel, the angel when the moon is almost full, has flowing robes of silver and gold. Be patient for just a few more days. Now is not the moment to reach out for what you want.

Jeduthan, angel of the evening and of the heavenly choirs, has an indigo halo and wings. Try to go home on time and not work too late at home at least three days a week.

Jehoel is the angel of diversity. Branch out and make small lifestyle changes, take breaks from routine, or learn a new language.

Jehudiel rules the planets, and has a halo of dark blue. A particularly lucky time for you to succeed lies ahead, so look out for an unusual opportunity or new person entering your life.

Jeliel, the orange blossom angel, presides over weddings and happy long-term commitments. It is time to ask for what you want, or be glad of what you have.

Jeremiel, archangel of rebirth and new beginnings, has purple and silver wings. Letting go of bad habits can be painful, but the energies of good change are all around you.

Johiel, angel of paradise on earth, has a halo of flowers and berries. Ask yourself what would make you truly happy. It may be totally attainable.

Jophiel, archangel of happiness, has a sun-bright orange halo. Smile today even if you do not feel like it and you will lift the mood of everyone you meet.

Kabshiel is a stately angel with white robes and whose wings shimmer with white light. Do not hold back from offering others your wisdom if you think they are making a mistake.

Kakabel, angel of the stars and constellations, has dark blue robes studded with stars and is surrounded by glowing light. Though we are influenced by cosmic energies, ultimately we must decide our destiny rather than leave it to fate.

Kutiel, angel of hidden water, minerals, and treasure, has iridescent wings and a burnished gold halo. Be alert to what is going on beneath the surface in a current work situation.

Lailah, angel of fertility, gives each newborn its special angel. She is surrounded by tiny angels and has full robes to enfold children and babies when they cry. Any issues regarding babies, children, and fertility or any concerns with your own mother are favoured.

Lauviah is the angel of those who are naturally talented in unconventional ways. Value your unique potential and worldview rather than follow others.

Lecabel, angel of food and mealtimes, has a wonderful smile. Rather than grazing or snacking, take time to enjoy the blessings of food, whether alone or with a family.

Lehahiah is the angel of restoring and maintaining balance, and carries golden scales and a golden scroll. Do not accept matters that irritate or frustrate you just because they have been that way for years.

Lelahel is a pale-green winged angel of love, family affection, and romance. Make time to be with people you care for or, if alone, seek new social connections.

Leuviah, the tall, white angel of the divine libraries of secret wisdom, says you should seek the advice of an older person or trusted source of knowledge.

Loquel is the angel who supports anyone who is not getting equal rights. Insist on respect and fair treatment if your efforts are not rewarded or appreciated.

Lumiel, archangel of Earth, holds a torch of light. Refuse to be panicked if people are demanding you keep to impossible schedules.

Machidiel or **Malchidiel** is the warrior angel, with sparkling golden-red halo and wings. Act confidently even if you are not, as this is a time to impress others and improve your status.

Mahasiah is a shadowy angel of mysteries, shrouded in pearly grey. Keep any secret knowledge to yourself and be careful who you confide in.

Maion is the angel of self-discipline and self-employment. Even if you are in a company, use your initiative. This is the time to further any ideas to work for yourself in the future.

Maktiel, angel of fruit and fruit trees, has wings of orange and lemon yellow. A sudden renewal of energy will flow through you. Use it to get back on track.

Manakiel, with sea-green robes, protects sea creatures and the oceans. A sudden hunch or premonition will prove accurate.

Manna is another angel of the food of the angels, occasionally offered to mortals. She is surrounded by flowers and butterflies. Do not settle for second best or compromise your dreams or ideals.

Mathariel and **Ridya,** twin angels of rain, have grey wings made of raindrops. Do not bottle up your feelings as you will feel happier once you have spoken your mind.

Mebahel is the angel of the fair distribution of resources. This is a good time to recover what you are owed, whether in money or favours.

Mebahiah is an angel of fertility in every sense. She wears creamy white robes and carries fruit and flowers. Do not worry about time passing. Trust, for there are still good times ahead to attain your desire for fertility in the way you most desire it.

Mehalel is the angel who draws a veil over past losses and betrayal. The past will not return, for this is a different situation you are entering.

Mehiel is the angel of writers and poets, especially struggling ones. We all have at least one book within us. Do not be discouraged from writing or creative expression.

Memumah, a misty silvery angel, is the sender of sleep and dreams. You will contact someone special in a dream if you say their name before sleep.

Menadel is the angel who blesses all far from home. You will find the right home if you have not already found the place you are meant to be.

Menor is the flamelike angel of candles. Light a candle tonight to connect with a far-away loved one or call someone back into your life.

Metatron, tallest of the archangels, guards the records of our destiny. Take your time to make the right decision about the future and if in doubt, wait.

Micah is the angel who oversees the blueprint of the world of nature and humanity. Focus on your longer-term future and avoid short-term diversions with instant results.

Michael or **Mikael** is a golden-winged archangel of the sun. Fight for what you know is right for yourself or a family member and you will win.

Mihael, angel of lasting loyalty and fidelity, has deep-green wings and halo. We all have a right to honesty and loyalty in any relationship, so if you have doubts, ask.

Mihr, angel of friendship, has the fragrance of roses. You will make a new friend who sees life as you do. Set up a get-together with old friends even if you are busy.

Mitzrael, angel of freedom of speech, wears rich blue robes and has very large blue wings. Speak out calmly but assertively rather than swallow anger or frustration; refuse to be silenced.

Moriel, Ruhiel, Rujiel, and **Ben Nez** are the ethereal Angels of the Four Winds. They are surrounded by swirling winds that blow petals and leaves around them as they fly. Stagnation will blow out of your life and slow matters will start moving if you make an effort now.

Mumiah is the pure, shining white angel of medicine. You need not worry about health for yourself or loved ones. However, do get a check up to reassure yourself if you are still anxious.

Muriel is the healer angel, with her magic carpet of dreams. Live your own dreams and not those imposed on you by others, however well meaning.

Nadiel, the angel of migration, wears rich purple. If you have itchy feet, this is a beneficial time for home moves, relocations, or even a home makeover.

Nahaliel is the misty-green angel of streams. Small steps lead to great results, but the first step is the hardest.

Nanael is the angel of scholarship and especially coping with disadvantages or disability. You can master a new skill or technology if you take it slowly and ask for help if necessary.

Nathaniel, the angel of forest fire, burns away what is no longer of use. Rise above pettiness and tunnel vision in others and if necessary, move on.

Natiel is the lilac angel of children and older people who are all in danger. These are dangerous times, but do not let fear prevent you from enjoying life to the full.

Neciel, angel of the waxing or increasing moon, has glowing golden wings. Take a chance and you will attract money, or money-spinning opportunities, into your life.

Nelchael, angel of ecological awareness and responsibility, wears robes of blue, green, and golden brown. Even a small step to reduce your carbon footprint makes a difference and may influence others.

Nemamiah is the angel who opens the gates of the new year with his brilliant light. A new beginning you might not have chosen will lead to a rewarding future life if you embrace the change.

Nephonos is the angel who runs swiftly through heaven and earth, scattering white feathers. A hectic time awaits, so make an all-out effort and forget leisure.

Nithaiah, angel of poets and prophecy, carries a silver scroll. Choose your words carefully and be tactful and you will get the result you desire.

Ochiel, angel of alchemy and transformation, has sparkling gems on his robes. You have everything you need for success, so why wait?

Ofaniel, an archangel of the rotating moon, has one hundred pairs of silver wings. Focus on the bigger picture and let the precise details sort themselves out.

Omael, angel of different cultures and languages, wears dark-blue robes. Do not allow narrow-mindedness in others to stop you from finding happiness your own way.

Oranir is the golden angel of midsummer. Make yourself happy today and forget tomorrow or yesterday.

Oreus is an angel made of light beams, who assisted the Creation. Whatever you create—poetry, a lovely garden, a successful business or a happy home—do it wholeheartedly.

Oriel is a female angel who helps mothers and children and all who need nurturing. We all need some TLC, so for once act helpless and let others care for you.

Orifiel, angel of the wilderness, soars on his huge cloudy wings. Plan a fun outdoors day or weekend soon, even if it is freezing outside.

Ormazd, angel of light and goodness, leads the way with his golden torch. If you want a promotion or to be in the spotlight, now is the time.

Osgaebial, a messenger angel, is followed by hosts of angels. Try to track down an old friend or family member with whom you have lost touch, but who is in your thoughts.

Othias, an angel of treasure, has robes that glisten with tiny natural gems. An unexpected bonus or gift will come your way. Send a present or card to someone you value.

Ouestucati, an angel with soft white hands, welcomes strangers. Ask someone who is lonely to lunch or coffee. They may prove good company.

Padael, an angel of deliverance, bears a golden sword and shield. Have you received one too many nasty letters or memos? Seek advice from an expert or get support rather than suffer in silence.

Pahaliah, an angel of trust, has a halo of pale lilac and wings of deep purple. Do not give up on what seems a hopeless cause or situation—you can eventually turn it round.

Pesagniyah is the angel who looks into a shadowy crystal at the past and the future. Some past venture or acquaintance could hold the key to unlocking the future.

Phul, angel of still waters, has silvery blue robes. Empty your mind of irrelevant concerns and avoid time-wasters.

Poiel, the scarlet-robed angel, rules over philosophy and good luck. Good fortune is coming your way through past efforts you made that you had given up on.

Proenia is the pure white light angel who helped to create Adam and Eve. No one or nothing is perfect, so don't throw out the baby with the bathwater.

Qaphsiel, a moon angel, says be extra careful with your possessions as you may be prone to losing something of value in your haste.

Rachiel, angel of all loving relationships, has wings and a halo of deep pink. Do not let outside interference affect relationships or the pursuit of love.

Radueriel is leader of the angelic horsemen. A quick, impulsive decision may bring swift changes, which may be what you want or need.

Raguel, archangel of ice and snow, has a halo of icicles. Coldness will melt but you may have changed and no longer want the person back in your life.

Rahab, angel of the sea, wears robes of swirling blue and green. Something precious or vital you have lost or misplaced will be returned.

Rampel, angel of mountains, has wings of silver mist. You can and must go on right now—even if you are tired, you will get through.

Raphael is archangel of all healers and healing. You naturally heal many people as you talk to them and may someday want to develop your healing powers.

Raziel is misty archangel of mysteries. The way is not clear, so you may have to take a leap of faith.

Rehael is the angel of good health and long life. He wears white robes and carries vials of healing oils. A reassuring angel about any health worries for you and older family members.

Reiliel is angel of idealism and altruism at work. Your integrity is your greatest strength—do not compromise it, however tempting instant rewards may seem.

Remiel or **Remliel** is archangel of thunder. People may be making a lot of noise, but these are largely empty threats, so ignore them.

Requiel is angel of the late waning moon. A good time to give up a habit that is bad for your health and see less of those who encourage it.

Rismuch is the angel of cultivated land and crop growth, clothed in golden brown. What you start now will, if you continue to nurture it, bring results within six months.

Rochel is an angel who finds lost people and animals as well as possessions. He carries a traveller's staff and a golden torch. You may hear good news after you had given up all hope.

Sabriel, "the brilliant one," is the archangel of overcoming challenges. Yes, your idea is a good one, so use it before someone else does.

Sachiel, archangel of the harvest and prosperity, has blue and purple wings. There is a chance to take the lead or shine unexpectedly.

Sachluph, angel of flowers and herbs, has wings of white petals. Have flowers at work or in the home for harmony and fragrance.

Safriel is a guardian angel who drives away malevolence with a golden sword. Watch out for someone deliberately trying to provoke you, and do not take the bait.

Sahaliah is the angel of vegetables. Nothing is too trivial for attention if it matters to someone, so do not feel you are wasting your time in helping.

Sakmakiel is the archer angel, with a silver bow and gold-tipped arrows. You may feel especially sensitive around others today, with good reason.

Salatheel or **Salathiel** is the angel who protected Adam and Eve after the Fall. "No" does not mean no forever, so present a scheme or approach to a person in another way another day.

Salilus is the angel who opens locked doors with his golden key. A group or organisation that has excluded you may open its doors.

Samael or **Sammael,** archangel of truth, has dark blue wings. Look sceptically at someone's claims of apparently great achievements and qualifications.

Samandriel, angel of imagination, has multicoloured wings. Picture what you most want and you will bring it closer to reality with every visualisation.

Sandalphon, angel of children and teaching, stands tall in shimmering robes of stars. Even a seemingly unpromising situation will bring valuable experience and new skills.

Sariel is the archangel who turns the wheel of the astrological year. Do not fight against or mourn the passing of time, but welcome each new stage.

Seheiah or **Sealiah,** angel of hygiene and the kitchen, has a halo of lilies. If you are often unwell, you may have a minor food or chemical allergy, so take steps to remedy this.

Seraphiel or **Serapiel** is the seeing angel. What we do is more important than what we promise or plan. Value people of action.

Sereda, the female healing angel, has soft apricot-coloured wings. New members of the family through remarriage or new partnerships may have divided loyalties. Be patient, but set your limits.

Shalgiel is the angel of snow, shimmering with frost and icicles. Today may not be the best time to make a request of others.

Shamshiel is angel of the light of day, whose halo and wings are like sunrise. Find something positive to say if everyone else is being negative or supercritical.

Shekinah, angel of the heart of any home, carries a white candle. Light a candle when you return home or in the early morning and draw peace around you.

Sitael, the angel who overcomes any hardship, carries the heavy burdens of all who need help. Better times are ahead, but learn to say no to unreasonable demands.

Sofiel, farming angel, has a golden brown halo. Security matters right now. Do not make rash decisions or give up because someone or something seems unexciting.

Sophia is angel of wisdom, clothed in pure white. You are precious and special. Welcome the day and take your rightful place.

Soqed Hozi, angel of partners and partnerships in love and business, is brilliant in red and gold. In any encounter, try to find common ground, even if empathy does not come instantly.

Su'iel is the angel who guards against earthquakes and natural disasters. He wears sandy yellows and clay-earth red, and carries a huge staff with a serpent head with which he strikes the earth. If you rarely show anger over trivial matters, people will take you seriously when you do erupt.

Susabo, angel of voyagers and explorers, has a golden banner streaming in the wind. Adventures can occur close to home, so explore your local region like a tourist.

Tabris, angel of free will, stands at the crossroads of destiny. He is a tall angel who can see the past, present, and future. Decide whether to move forward, go back, or stay where you are for now. But make a decision.

Tagriel, angel of the waning crescent moon, is almost transparent with silvery grey hair and a single star on her halo. Are you holding on to something or someone out of habit or worry about being alone?

Taharial, angel of purification, is snow white and shimmers with light. Establish your boundaries, making it clear that unhelpful suggestions or backbiting is no longer acceptable.

Temeluch is the pale-pink angel who cares for children. She laughs a lot and is very light and delicate, almost elfinlike. If you have children, a worry will be resolved. If not, let your inner child out for some fun.

Tharsis, the angel of clean drinking water, has a crystal halo and wings. It's time to leap into life and not stand on the sidelines.

The angel clothed with the sun, who has no name, has the moon under her feet and wears a crown of stars. You care for the world. Who cares for you?

Torquaret is the golden-brown angel of autumn and of resolving legal and personal claims. What is rightfully yours will eventually come to you.

Trgiaob is the angel of wild birds, bees and butterflies. Free yourself from self-imposed restrictions and say "yes," not "maybe one day."

Trsiel is angel of rivers, with a halo of sparkling water drops. The river is flowing and it may be time to try out that creative venture in the public marketplace.

Tubiel, angel of lost birds and animals, has shimmering golden wings. If something or someone is clearly not coming back, move on.

Uriel is archangel of inner fire and the earth. Be courageous and do not wait to be invited to join in with life.

Urim is the angel who determines human destiny. This is a time to rewrite history using what you know now. It may not be too late to find the way back.

Uwula, angel of eclipses of the sun and moon, has a silver veil. Do not fear uncertainty, for if everything remained the same, we would never move forward.

Vael, another angel of peace, brings a truce in conflict situations. He is silvery grey and radiates calm and harmony. Do not commit yourself to what you will regret just to keep the peace or buy time.

Vasairiah is another angel of justice and rights. He is an older-looking angel with a large golden book, which he carries open in his hands. Do not let a difficult neighbour spoil your domestic peace. Conciliate, but do not be bullied.

Vehuel is the angel of creativity. He has orange wings and long golden robes. Everyone can be creative, so develop this side of yourself in your own way, whether for pleasure or profit.

Vehuiah is angel of the dawn of the spring. He has a lemon-yellow halo and wings that look like early morning spring sunlight. Accept that some people are never pleased or face the truth. Please yourself for a change.

Verchiel or **Verachiel** is the golden joy bringer. Unless you are happy and fulfilled you cannot bring happiness to others.

Veuliah is the angel of compromise and fairness. He wears silvery grey robes and has soft grey wings and a misty halo. Walk away, even temporarily, from a destructive person or situation so you are not sucked in by their negativity.

Vohumanah, angel of positive thought, sheds light as he walks. Before making an irrevocable snap judgment, listen to both sides of the story.

Yahriel, angel of the moon phases, shines like a pale moon with silver shimmers in his halo. Get back in touch with your natural inner rhythms and energy peaks and ebbs to escape from life's relentless 24/7 pace.

Yehudiah is the angel of overcoming grief and loss. He wears shimmering black robes and has a misty grey halo and wings, and has a very kind, gentle expression. Mourn for whatever or whoever is gone from your life rather than denying your natural feelings.

Yeiayel, with the twinkling eyes, is the angel of loving companionship. Throw an impromptu informal party and invite everyone you know to mix in.

Yeratel is a light bringer and golden defender of liberty. Be realistic about what you can achieve in righting an injustice rather than letting bitterness eat away at you.

Yushamin, female angel of prosperity, carries a basket of grain. She promises you will acquire a much sought-after possession at a really good price.

Zaafiel is the angel of spring rain. Making a change in one area of your daily world will revitalise other parts of your life.

Zaamiel, protector angel of fierce winds, travels in swirls of cloud. You are right on this occasion. Do not let anyone convince you otherwise.

Zacharel is archangel of spiritual rather than physical gold. Do not let someone who is very materialistic make you feel inadequate.

Zachriel, angel of memory, wears robes of violet. Store up good memories and experiences and make yourself happy, even in a small way every day.

Zadkiel, archangel of abundance and alternative healing, has sky-blue wings. If you feel overwhelmed, stop and meditate, walk, or relax for a few minutes to regain your equilibrium.

Zagveron is the angel of purity and salt. Avoid people who encourage you to take risks or live an unhealthy or stressful lifestyle.

Zagzagel is the angel who appeared to Moses in the burning bush. For now you accept the status quo, however restrictive or unreasonable—things will change.

Zikiel, angel of comets and meteors, is a dazzling angel of light. Aim high, even if others say it will never happen. You will surprise them all.

Zuphlas is the angel of the forests. He wears pine green and carries a golden axe, cutting back the trees when they grow too dense, and cares for the wildlife that make their homes in the forest. Right now you may feel unable to see a way through the work mountain. Step back and you will see steady progress.

Zuriel, angel who prevents humans from doing impulsive, stupid things, has pale-blue wings and halo and has beautiful hands that comfort all who are in trouble through their own mistakes. We all get tempted. Ask yourself if the consequences are worth it. If so, go ahead.

INDEX